# GREAT ART AND ARTISTS OF THE WORLD

# BRITISH AND NORTH AMERICAN ART TO 1900

GREAT ART AND ARTISTS OF THE WORLD

# BRITISH AND NORTH AMERICAN ART TO 1900

Edited, with an Introduction, by

Dr. Kenneth Garlick

*Lecturer in History of Art and Deputy Director,*
*Barber Institute of Fine Arts, Birmingham, England*

FRANKLIN WATTS, INC.

A Division of Grolier Incorporated

575 LEXINGTON AVENUE, NEW YORK 10022

# HOW TO USE THIS BOOK

To obtain the maximum information and interest from this series it is necessary to understand its basic plan. With the exception of the first and last volumes, which are more general in their scope, each of the other eight volumes is arranged as follows:

First, a historical Introduction sets out the main lines of development within the school or period, with special reference to the major artists and the major works of art.

This is followed by a biographical section outlining the life and work of every major artist and important minor artists. The Biographies run in alphabetical order according to the name by which each artist is most generally known, whether it be surname, or Christian name (as for example LEONARDO da Vinci), or nickname (as TINTORETTO). With each biography is given a cross-reference to the page or pages on which he is represented in the plates sections which follow; a monochrome reproduction of one or more of his other works; and (where possible) a self-portrait or portrait of the artist and a specimen of his signature.

Next follow the sections of Color Plates, Drawings, and Sculpture. Each of these sections is arranged in chronological order according to the date of the artist's birth, though in a few cases minor adjustments to this order have been made for the sake of comparison or design. To illustrate painting techniques, particularly of frescoes and large easel paintings, some color plates show a detail rather than the whole work; but the use of such a detail is indicated in the caption, and a monochrome illustration of the whole work is normally given with the artist's biography; in such cases the size given in the caption refers to the whole painting. The location of every work of art is included in its caption. Every effort has been made to include also the size, medium, and date of each work represented in the plates, though this has not always been possible since not every museum has such information available for all the items in its collection. The reader will also appreciate that the precise dating of many works of art is the subject of scholarly controversy; however, no dates have been included here unless they have the authority of qualified experts and art historians.

A final section, entitled Influences and Developments, rounds off the volume by drawing together the main ideas and characteristics of schools and styles, and by exploring the internal and external influences that have made their impact on the development of the arts during the period concerned.

A list of basic reference books for further reading appears on page 16. Books containing material of special interest concerning an individual artist are listed at the end of the relevant biography.

To avoid repetitive explanation of basic technical terms such as *genre, chiaroscuro, baroque*, etc., an illustrated Glossary is provided in the volume entitled *How to Look at Art*. Also in that volume is an Index listing every artist mentioned throughout the series.

Taken as a whole, the series thus provides a comprehensive, carefully integrated, and highly informative survey of the achievement and significance of Western Art from its origins to the present day.

NOTE.—The terminal dates in the titles of some of the volumes are inevitably approximate. One volume will sometimes overlap with another. Certain artists mentioned under French Art, for example, are also represented under the Impressionists, and the Post-Impressionists merge imperceptibly with the Moderns. In the ever-continuous process of Art it is difficult to contain schools or periods within precise boundaries.

Library of Congress Catalog Card Number: 65-10268
Copyright (©) 1965 by Grolier Incorporated
Also published 1965 by Grolier Incorporated under the title of *The Book of Art*

Designed and produced by George Rainbird Ltd., London
PRINTED IN ITALY by Amilcare Pizzi S.p.A., Milan

# Contents

## ACKNOWLEDGMENTS

The publishers and producers wish to express their gratitude to all the museums, art galleries, collectors, photographers and agencies who have courteously assisted them in obtaining the material for the illustrations reproduced in this volume. They would especially like to thank the following:

Thos. Agnew & Sons Ltd., London
The Albany Institute of History of Art, New York
The Alte Pinakothek, Munich
Archives Photographiques, Paris
The Art Institute, Chicago
The Art Museum, Worcester, Mass.
The Arts Council of Great Britain, London
The Ashmolean Museum, Oxford, England
The Atheneum, Boston, Mass.
The Bancroft Foundation, Wilmington, Del.
The Trustees of the Barber Institute of Fine Arts,
    Birmingham, England
The Beaverbrook Art Gallery, Fredericton, N.B., Canada
The Trustees of the British Museum, London

The Brooklyn Museum, New York
Caisse Nationale des Monuments Historiques, Paris
The Cecil Higgins Museum, Bedford, England
The Trustees of the Chatsworth Settlement, Chatsworth,
    England
The Cincinnati Art Museum, Ohio
The City Art Gallery, Bristol, England
The City Art Gallery, Glasgow
The City Art Gallery, Leeds, England
The City Art Museum, St. Louis, Mo.
The City Museum and Art Gallery, Birmingham, England
The Cleveland Museum of Art, Ohio
Messrs. P. and D. Colnaghi & Co., London
The Governors of the Thomas Coram Foundation for
    Children, London
The Corcoran Art Gallery, Washington, D.C.
The Courtauld Institute, London
The Courtauld Institute Galleries, University of London
Edmark Studio, Oxford, England
The Syndics of the Fitzwilliam Museum, Cambridge, England
The Fogg Art Museum, Cambridge, Mass.
Mr. Brinsley Ford, London
The Free Public Library, Worcester, Mass.

6

## ABBREVIATIONS

| | |
|---|---|
| in. | inches |
| St. | Saint (English and German) |
| St. or Ste. | Saint (French) |
| S. | Saint (Italian and Spanish) |
| Acad. | Academy |
| Ashmolean | Ashmolean Museum, Oxford, England |
| B.M. | British Museum, London |
| Cath. | Cathedral |
| Coll. | Collection |
| Fitzwm. | Fitzwilliam Museum, Cambridge, England |
| Gall. | Gallery |
| Hist. Soc. | Historical Society, New York |
| Inst. | Institute |
| Met. Mus. | Metropolitan Museum of Art, New York |
| Mus. | Museum |
| N.G. | National Gallery, London |
| N.G. of Canada | National Gallery of Canada, Ottawa |
| N.G. of Scotland | National Gallery of Scotland, Edinburgh |
| N.P.G. | National Portrait Gallery, London |
| Nat. Maritime Mus. | National Maritime Museum, Greenwich, London |
| Pal. | Palace |
| R.A. | Royal Academy, London |
| Royal Coll. | Royal Collection, England |
| Tate | Tate Gallery, London |
| V. and A. | Victoria and Albert Museum, London |

# Introduction

## British and North American Art to 1900

The art of easel painting developed late in England. The Renaissance of all the arts in Italy was at that stage of its history known as Mannerism—in some respects a period of decline—when Hans Holbein paid his first visit to London in 1526. Architecture and sculpture had of course achieved independent triumphs in English churches and cathedrals and church monuments long before this, and wall painting in churches, although it was provincial, was at least a flourishing art with a history behind it. But easel painting was almost non-existent. Sets of portraits of the kings of England, of very indifferent workmanship, were turned out for great houses towards the end of the 15th century, but few portraits of living persons other than the king were ever painted. Henry VII was in fact the first English monarch to employ a painter of any standing to take his likeness, Miguel Sithium the Fleming (p. 210). It was he also who received as a gift from the Duke of Urbino the first fine Italian painting ever to reach England, Raphael's little *St. George and the Dragon* (p. 215), which is now in the National Gallery at Washington.

### Holbein

Henry VIII, who was a man of some taste and culture, was well aware that his court could not compare in sophistication, let alone magnificence, with the courts of Europe, and, in particular, with that of his political rival, Francis I of France; and when in 1532 Holbein paid a second visit to London the king realized that here was an artist of European standing who could probably enhance his own reputation abroad, and took him into his service a few years later. Holbein's method of portraiture, linear, detailed, and decorative, was related to what is now known as the international court style. François Clouet at the court of France and Agnolo Bron-

zino at the court of the Medici in Florence worked in a rather similar manner; but there was no one in England who could compare with Holbein, and although at various times later in the century other European painters of repute worked in England—Eworth, Mor, and Zuccaro—the Holbein manner was dominant until the death of Queen Elizabeth.

### Miniature painting

During the second half of the 16th century there must have been work for a large number of portrait painters, but we can identify only a few of them by name and only a very few have a personal style that can easily be recognized. It may be that the personalities and achievements of the visiting foreigners inhibited the native artist; it is more likely that his talent was quite undeveloped and that the whole concept of painting in oils—at this time usually on panel—was too new for him to assimilate it quickly. And so it is not surprising that the only native painter of genius in the 16th century was Nicholas Hilliard, the miniaturist. The art of painting in miniature on vellum had been perfected in the monasteries, and it was not likely that it would be lost overnight with their dissolution in 1539. Illuminated books were no longer produced for the church, but the tradition of illumination was carried on by the painter of miniature portraits. Hilliard recorded the human face with all Holbein's accuracy but with less complete detachment. His interpretation is more intimate and more sensitive, and his sitters often look as if they were born to compose, or to receive in homage, the courtly lyrics of the day.

Elizabeth I did very little to encourage the arts. Her portrait was painted a great many times, but she made it clear that what she wanted was a royal image, not a likeness. She did not relish an exact representation of her aging features, and in her time the royal portrait became a set costume piece. In fact portraiture in general under Elizabeth and under her successor James I was a record of clothes as much as of faces. The lace collars, the embroidered bodices and jackets and trunks, the elaborate stockings and shoes, hide the real personality from us. Cornelius Johnson and Daniel Mytens, who were young men in the reign of James, did something to give the face its proper place as the subject of a portrait; but it was van Dyck who transformed the art of portraiture in England and with it English painting.

## Van Dyck

Van Dyck came over from Antwerp to London in 1620 and entered the service of James I, but he left for Italy in 1621 and did not return to England until 1632, when James had been dead some years. He then became court painter to Charles I, and, apart from an unsuccessful visit to the Continent in 1640, made London his home and headquarters until his death in 1641. Van Dyck had lived in Genoa and in Rome and had traveled to other parts of Italy. He admired and was greatly influenced by Venetian painting and by Titian in particular, and when he settled in London he had in Charles I a patron who was also an ardent and inspired collector. In the royal palaces he could see Titians of the first quality, the Mantegna *Triumphs of Caesar* (p. 215), the Raphael cartoons for the Vatican tapestries, and many other fine works of art. The court of Charles was as learned, as sophisticated, as elegant as any in Europe. Intellectually it was perhaps the liveliest. Van Dyck never felt the least desire to leave it, and the King had no desire to lose him, and for the first time since Holbein, pictures were painted in London by a European master of the first rank. They were not strictly English paintings, as van Dyck was not an Englishman, but William Dobson, who worked for a time in his studio, produced portraits to be compared in quality with van Dyck's own, and one may say that apart from the 16th-century miniaturists Dobson was the first native painter of considerable stature to appear.

## The van Dyck tradition

Van Dyck brought much more than elegance to the English portrait. It is true that he presented the members of the court and of the aristocracy as if they were embodiments of grace and noble bearing, and they could not all have possessed the refinement of build and feature which his canvases suggest; but he had, in addition to this sense of style, a true capacity for revealing personality. Van Dyck's subjects are persons, and their portraits are the work of a master who created in them an image which has passed down to history as the type of all that an English aristocrat should be. Reynolds, Gainsborough, Lawrence, and a host of portrait painters down to Sargent and de Laszlo continued to perpetuate the van Dyck tradition.

## The dominance of foreign painters

Unfortunately William Dobson died in 1646, only five years after van Dyck himself, and the successor to the major portrait practice was a Dutchman, Peter Lely. The Civil War made anything but a sporadic development in any of the arts impossible, but Lely succeeded in establishing himself, working for both sides, and after the Restoration he became court painter to Charles II. His work appears to be uneven in quality, largely because his portraits exist in so many versions. The name Lely on a frame or in a catalogue often indicates no more than that the picture issued from his studio or follows his design; a portrait painted entirely by his own hand is with few exceptions vigorous and impressive. He was less refined than van Dyck, but he had a similar sense of style and he was aware of European Baroque art. He lived in London until his death in 1680. During this time a number of able British portrait painters emerged, but even so the visiting foreigners still took the lead. It was a German, Godfrey Kneller, who became a favorite painter of Queen Anne and later of George I.

The 18th century saw enormous changes. Until then the portrait had been the English painter's main preoccupation. Now the arts of landscape painting and of history painting also began to flourish: indeed, history painting eventually gained in prestige over portraiture. And at last the visiting foreigner took second place.

## Hogarth

It was William Hogarth who took what amounted to a political line in asserting that the time had come when the English painter was at least as good as the foreigner. After the death of Kneller in 1723, first Amigoni and then van Loo had paid long visits to England and had stolen the portrait market. They had been trained to use with ease all the apparatus of the European Baroque portrait: stylized folds and flutters of clothes and draperies, decorative backgrounds of columns, curtains, loops, and tassels. But Hogarth knew that he was just as capable of doing this sort of thing as they were. Moreover, he knew that he had other and more important things to say and that it was not in portraiture that his real interest or his real gift lay. He was a born illustrator. He was also a born moralist, a fighter for causes, and he found exactly the right mode of expression for his genius in the moral narrative picture. He would invent a story and tell it in a succession of scenes, six or eight at the most, which he would paint on a comparatively small scale. He would then make engravings from the pictures, which are packed with lively detail and are, besides, the work of a man of intellect.

Hogarth, however, had great ambitions. He had worked under Sir James Thornhill, who carried out the painted decorations in the dome of St. Paul's and at Greenwich, the only native Baroque paintings of any quality in the country, and he himself painted large-scale decorations (though on a much smaller scale than Thornhill's) at St. Bartholomew's Hospital. He aspired to the creation of historical and religious pictures in what was then described as the Grand Manner. He wrote a treatise on the theory of painting, and in his self-portrait (p. 98) his palette is inscribed with the serpentine line of grace — by which he intends to show us that he affiliates himself to the classical tradition. It would probably have disappointed him to know that today we esteem most highly the topical narratives and the conversation pieces, which he would have regarded as ephemeral.

## The Royal Academy

The 18th century was the great age of looking back to the classical past. That indeed was its strength. It never even considered the fallacy, so widely accepted today, that constant changes are inevitable and must be accepted, and it was fortunate in that it knew nothing about speed in locomotion. In the field of the arts the intellectual traditionalism of the century was symbolized by the founding of the Royal Academy in 1768. Academies of painting, sculpture, and architecture had existed in many continental cities for a century or more, and their business was the training of artists and the teaching and discussion of the history of art and of art theories from ancient times onwards. The Royal Academy in London combined these functions with the holding of an annual exhibition which showed the work of its elected members and of those persons who submitted their entries to a selection committee. This annual exhibition soon became a feature of the London social year and remains so to this day, the difference being that it then represented the work of almost every British artist of standing, whereas today that is not so. The art world then was small and homogeneous.

## Reynolds

The first President of the Academy, Sir Joshua Reynolds, was an intellectual painter. He had spent two years in Italy, and he was a dedicated student of the art of the past. In his portrait compositions he paid homage to the Italian High Renaissance, to France, and to antique sculpture, and his references to or borrowings from Raphael or Veronese or the *Apollo Belvedere* (p. 221) were instantly admired and recognized. The "Discourses" which he addressed annually to the students of the Academy were written with polish, were widely read, and are accepted now, as they were then, as an important statement of artistic theory. Reynolds believed that portrait painting, which was his own profession, was after all only a secondary branch of the art. He believed that the Grand Manner should be emulated by every student; and by the Grand Manner he meant historical compositions of idealized human forms, high-minded, noble, owing a profound debt to the study, either from the originals or from engravings, of the frescoes and easel paintings of Raphael and Michelangelo and their contemporaries, of the Venetians, and of the antique sculpture in the Vatican Gallery. His learning and his advice were sound but were ill-suited to the temperament of his students. The Grand Manner does not come naturally to the Englishman, whose gift is usually more intimate and less ambitious in character, and Sir Joshua's precepts were responsible for the production of a great deal of serious but not very exciting painting which is now of interest chiefly to the historian. His vindication is his own work.

## Gainsborough

There could have been no greater contrast to Reynolds than his only serious rival, Thomas Gainsborough. Gainsborough was as natural a painter as Reynolds was a painter formed by study. He never went abroad. He was not an intellectual. He was no consistent student of the art of the past, although he enormously admired van Dyck and made occasional copies of Murillo and Salvator Rosa and Rembrandt and Rubens. He employed no assistants to paint the draperies in his portraits, as was then the usual custom. He was a fine, spontaneous draftsman, whereas Reynolds drew rather clumsily. Moreover he had as great a love of landscape painting as of portraiture, and remarked that had he not to earn a living he would abandon the portrait altogether. Gainsborough was indeed, with Richard Wilson, one of the two master landscape painters of the century. In the preceding century there had been some landscape painting—John Wootton, who began working in the 1690's, really counts as an 18th-century man—but it amounts to very little. Wilson and Gainsborough represent the two types of landscape painting that emerged after 1700.

## The beginnings of landscape painting

Wilson spent some time in Italy and there became imbued with the spirit of Claude. His Italian landscapes are composed according to the Claudian formula, with framing "wings" of foliage and with the eye led by devious paths and streams across an expanse of country to a golden horizon. When he returned to England he adapted this formula to a different scene; and the English country house painted by him in its parkland setting often has a faintly Italian air about it. Gainsborough in contrast had no special feeling for things Italian. His first loves were the Dutch painters, Ruisdael and Hobbema and Wynants, and his earliest records of the Suffolk scene are worked out as minutely to the Dutch pattern of rutted paths and leafy woods as were Wilson's to the Claudian panorama. But he fairly soon evolved his own very free method of dealing with sweeps of branch and foliage and the spread of meadow and

hillside. In fact, when he no longer had time to walk into the country to take notes he composed imaginary landscapes from pieces of twig and moss and glass and grit arranged by the light of a candle on a table in his studio: and his knowledge of the natural scene was so accurate, his love of nature so keen and lively, that these "artificial" landscapes are as fresh and real as any he ever painted. They are of course the antithesis of the painstaking, accurate recording of picturesque scenes or ruins which form the subject-matter of the topographical painting in watercolor, done for the engraver, that was produced to a high quality in bulk throughout the century. Such work was however of vital importance to the development of watercolor painting as an art. Paul Sandby and, a little later, J. R. Cozens remained professional topographical artists while, almost incidentally, they demonstrated that watercolors could be used on a scale and to an effect comparable with those of oils.

Gainsborough was very much on his own in not having traveled and in taking little notice of Italy and Italian painting, for it had become increasingly fashionable and increasingly easy for the English painter to spend a year or more of his youth abroad. The Grand Tour of Europe which had been made occasionally by Englishmen of fashion from the 16th century onwards now became the rage. Not only did Grand Tourists collect old masters on their travels and buy paintings which recorded the places they had visited: they sometimes took a painter with them. Or more often the painter would travel on his own and earn his keep by taking commissions from the tourists when he got to Rome or Florence or Naples. It was now also that American artists first came to study in Europe. In the 1760's Rome was a great center of Classical and Neoclassical studies, not only for the monuments of the Roman Empire which it had to show but also because the German scholar Winckelmann and his compatriot Mengs the painter were living in the city and collaborated in propagating a revival of interest in the Antique. Their teachings had a profound influence, even attracting young artists from across the Atlantic.

## American painters in Europe

Benjamin West of Pennsylvania came to Rome in 1760. John Singleton Copley of Boston followed in 1774.

Both eventually settled in London, and although they both practiced portrait painting they led the field in the new genre of history painting. West even caused a sensation by painting *The Death of Wolfe* in contemporary dress, against the accepted rules of history painting as he had learned them in Rome. Another New Englander to go to London (in 1775) was Gilbert Stuart, who practiced exclusively as a portrait painter. Stuart returned to America to paint his famous portraits of George Washington and others, but Copley and West stayed on. West succeeded Reynolds as President of the Royal Academy in 1792. The American school developed very rapidly indeed from about this time, and any notion that it did so in isolation, out of touch with what was happening in Europe, is quite false. It must not, however, be overlooked that the American portrait painters of the first half of the 18th century, John Smibert (who had emigrated from Scotland), and Robert Feke, remained essentially provincial, if professional. And a new nation growing up quickly over a vast continent inevitably produced innumerable 'primitives' alongside the professionals. It has continued to do so down to Grandma Moses. Some of the early work to come into this category is quite remarkably telling, especially that produced in the frontier regions of America and Canada.

### The French Revolution and its effects

The French Revolution had its effect on the arts as on politics and on the whole way of life in Europe. It is not quite true to say that Romanticism came in with revolution. It was already on its way. But revolution implies liberation; and liberation in the sense of freedom in technique, in subject-matter, and in expression is a characteristic of Romantic painting. That is not to say that the English Romantic painters were political rebels. In most cases they were not. Nor did they wish to throw off the past. Constable, Turner, Lawrence, were all students of the old masters. Turner indeed was so devoted an admirer of Claude that he bequeathed two of his own pictures to the London National Gallery on condition that they were hung in the company of two Claudes. They were, however, two of his comparatively early works. Towards the end of his long life he recorded color, light, and form with such a purely sensuous distillation of the visible scene that the subject cannot immediately be re-

cognized from the title of the picture. Venice seen across the lagoon, or the ruin of some castle on the Rhine, are transformed into visions where sun and mist and the shimmer of light on water dissolve all tangible shapes in an abstraction of color. It is easy to see why Turner appealed to some of the French Impressionists later in the century. Monet, painting his famous water-lily decorations nearly seventy years after Turner's death, went no further in the free transcribing of nature into art than Turner had done himself. It would be quite wrong to say that he was imitating Turner, but there is no doubt that the Turners in the National Gallery, London, (which he saw in 1870) impressed him deeply.

Constable, whose records of the English country scene are so fresh and vigorous, was also working things out in his own way, an entirely new way. He too admired the older masters. He sometimes used the Claudian devices of composition, and he learned a good deal from studying the landscapes of Rubens, but his approach was new in that it demanded a familiarity with nature resulting from hours and days of concentrated observation of tree-formation, cloud-formation, and cloud-movement, and of shadows shifting on fields and slopes. Not even Gainsborough was as devoted to the countryside as Constable. He felt no desire to travel as Turner did. He did not have Turner's capacity for translating nature in terms of romantic color-visions. Yet the passion of his observation is romantic, and so is the brightness of his palette. When he exhibited at the Paris salon in 1824 the young Delacroix placed a laurel wreath on the frame of *The Hay-Wain* (p. 232).

It may seem at first sight that Lawrence is a traditionalist in portrait painting compared with Constable and Turner and their contributions to the art of painting landscapes. It is true that he was fettered by the past in a way that Constable and Turner were not, because he could never quite forget that the public expected him to assume the mantle of Reynolds. He was not an artist of Constable's or Turner's stature, but he was of a rarer caliber than has usually been recognized and he gave new life to the academic portrait. He was a finer draftsman than any earlier English portrait painter with the exception of Gainsborough, and he had a tremendous natural gift for sheer lively painting. There is power in the sketch of William Lock (p. 124), which is less intellectual than a Reynolds, less poetic than a Gainsborough, less suave than a Romney, but is one of the few British portraits of the day that could hold its own beside a Goya.

## Provincial art in England

This is perhaps the place to make the point that by the year 1800 the number of persons earning a living in England by the art of painting was very large and was growing larger all the time. This was partly, of course, the result of the growth of the prosperity of the country and with it of the population. It was also partly due to the success of the Royal Academy, which encouraged the setting-up of exhibiting societies in many of the provincial cities. It is however very difficult for us to remember how slow communications were in those days and how much less individuals traveled about than they do today. Partly for this reason local societies produced local schools of painting which were truly provincial, growing out of their surroundings and belonging to them and not too much affected by what was happening in London. The most celebrated of them all, the Norwich School, has a place in the national picture. John Crome, its leader, brought the same freshness and vitality to the best of his paintings of the country around Norwich as Constable did to his paintings of Suffolk, but the work of Crome is characterized by an almost tangible earthiness which makes Constable's seem sophisticated by comparison.

## The English Romantics

Constable, Turner, Lawrence, intensely English though they are, all have a place in the European Romantic movement. Their work was hailed in France in its own time. Richard Parkes Bonington spent most of his very short working life in France and was a friend of Delacroix. On the other hand the French have never really taken to Blake or to his follower Samuel Palmer, whereas the English themselves tend nowadays to venerate both of them perhaps unduly. They are English to a fault, romantic to the point where art and life and religion are one. Blake all his life—as was not so with Palmer—refused to be persuaded by facts and by reality. He did not admit even the possibility that his convictions might be wrong. He was passionately logical when working out his own belief in the true and the absolutely honest, blindly illogical when applying it to daily life. In his paintings and drawings the same is true. He can and does ignore the academic rules as he pleases, but it is only when he ignores them with the most complete confidence that his design and his message tell supremely well. It is perhaps this splendid lack of logic that makes Blake a great Romantic. In the work of Palmer the issues are altogether more limited. He is concerned with the poetical, mystical interpretation of the pastoral landscape. Blake's shining vision of the Stars of the Morning singing together is confined by Palmer to the cornfields and the moonlit, wooded slopes of the Darent valley; but within these limits he created small painted lyrics of a rapturous nature.

## The Pre-Raphaelite Brotherhood

It is very understandable that the young Pre-Raphaelites looked back to Blake when they hoped to revive in English painting the pure spirit which they believed had inspired the painters of Italy before the time of Raphael. The Pre-Raphaelite movement was initiated in 1848, the year of revolution in Europe. Its members were very young men, Millais, Rossetti, and Holman Hunt being the most important of the original seven. After the death of Lawrence in 1830 the Royal Academy had had no member of European eminence, and while it would be untrue to say that its annual exhibitions were wholly mediocre, it is undeniable that the general standard and the choice of subject-matter were less high-minded than they had been in its early days. The young members of the Pre-Raphaelite Brotherhood, sensing this, wished to effect a change overnight. They sought truth to nature above all. They wished to preach sincerity, and they believed that their work would speak and demonstrate this message for them. When Millais painted *The Blind Girl* (p. 145) he set up his easel out of doors at Winchelsea so that he might observe and record with the utmost fidelity those beauties which the girl herself would never see, and might thus convey her tragedy more poignantly and truly. This same diligence directed the work of all the members of the P.R.B.—with the exception of Rossetti, who had neither the patience nor the same single-mindedness—and had a considerable influence on other painters, mostly young, who never actually joined the movement. Their sense of purpose never, perhaps, became quite as fanatical as Blake's, but it was that that linked the P.R.B. with the Romantic movement. It is a movement that one thinks of as extraordinarily and insularly English, partly because the P.R.B. pictures so often record with loving glowing accuracy the detail of the English landscape or garden or street. It had however a close counterpart in German Romantic painting earlier in the century, and it had an affinity with the sometimes clumsy realism of Courbet in France. American painters of the same years portray the natural scene with a similar intense delight, and the members of the P.R.B. would have responded warmly to the work of George Caleb Bingham.

By 1860 the Pre-Raphaelite movement had lost its impetus and was running to sentimentality. The aesthetic movement which succeeded it, typified by William Morris and Burne-Jones, was not yet in being, and the Royal Academy was only just building up to the immensely successful decades of the 1870's, 80's, and 90's, when enormous pictures of indifferent quality sold from its walls like hot cakes. The 1860's were quiet, and perhaps the best work produced in them was not painting but book-illustration.

This very summary account of what happened in three-hundred-and-fifty years cannot attempt to assess the characteristics of British painting as a whole or to discuss the question of whether indeed national characteristics exist and whether they remain permanent. The plates must provoke the questions and the answers in the minds of those who peruse them.

## The character of American painting

It is much easier to detect national characteristics in the painting produced in the United States and Canada in the hundred years 1760-1860. The North American painters saw things in a fresh and clear-cut way, as if the light in the New World gave to everything a sharper edge, as if they themselves were looking with their eyes wider open and with a more directly concentrated gaze than their contemporaries in Europe. They may have traveled to Europe and studied her traditions in the arts, but when they came to paint at home it was still all wonderfully new. Whether it is Copley recording the folds of the cheek of a prosperous Bostonian, or Charles Peale looking at himself, or Cole romanticizing extensive landscapes, or G. C. Bingham watching the busy life on a great river, the vitality of a young race immediately makes itself felt. This school of painting deserves to be more widely known and studied outside America than it is today. Almost all the best that it produced is now in American museums and for this reason makes an unforgettable impact on the visitor from Europe who is not really aware of what he is going to see. More should be known about the Hudson River School. The term is applied rather loosely to a number of painters working during the period 1820 to 1870 who did not necessarily know each other or think of themselves as belonging to a "school" but who chose for their subjects landscapes of a panoramic nature, river valleys, mountain valleys, river plains. Thomas Cole (p. 155), Asher Durand (p. 239), and later Albert Bierstadt and the early George Inness had the gift of conveying the grandeurs of the natural scene while they painted the details of it with painstaking fidelity. Bingham and W. S. Mount were more interested in the human activities to which the vastnesses of nature were a background, and a picture like Bingham's *Fur Traders Descending the Missouri* (p. 157) equates the transient business of man and the everlastingness of nature with a strong simplicity that is rarely found in European painting of the time. This unabashed simplicity is characteristic of the painting of the New World.

## Canadian painting

It is apparent also but with greater naïveté in Canadian painting of the same period, especially in the work of Paul Kane and Cornelius Krieghoff (p. 159); but painting in Canada lagged very far behind the States. The accomplished work of Antoine Plamondon (p. 158) was exceptional. It was not until after 1860 that something like a Canadian school began to form and an artist appeared like Robert Harris, who may be compared with the bigger names among the late 19th-century painters in the United States.

# Biographies

## SOME BOOKS FOR FURTHER READING

E. K. Waterhouse, *Painting in Britain 1530-1790*, London (Pelican History of Art), 1953.

*Painting in England 1700-1850. The Collection of Mr. and Mrs. Paul Mellon*, Virginia, 1963.

M. Whinney and O. Millar, *English Art 1625-1714*, London, 1957

R. H. Wilenski, *English Painting*, London, 1933.

R. H. Hubbard, *An Anthology of Canadian Art*, Toronto, 1960.

J. Woodward, *A Picture History of British Painting*, London, 1962.

D. Sutton, *American Painting*, London, 1948.

E. P. Richardson, *Painting in America*, New York, 1956.

E. P. Richardson, *American Romantic Painting*, New York, 1944.

M. Whinney, *Sculpture in Britain 1530-1830*, London (Pelican History of Art), 1964.

SEE ALSO UNDER THE INDIVIDUAL BIOGRAPHIES

# WASHINGTON ALLSTON

*The most important early American Romantic painter*

Washington Allston was born in South Carolina in 1779 and was educated first in Newport and then at Harvard. He was to spend most of his life in Boston. Determined to have a thorough training as an artist, Allston traveled to London, staying there two years, and then lived in Paris from 1803 to 1804. There he mingled with contemporary painters and frequented the Louvre. In 1804 he visited Italy and was enchanted by Venetian painting, particularly admiring Titian, Veronese, and Tintoretto. Except for a short spell in America, Allston remained in Europe until 1818.

His paintings before his return to America were large, subjective canvases expressing a Romantic vision of nature and life, although the influence of classical art is also apparent. Allston was the first American painter to reveal the awe-inspiring grandeur of nature and to explore the resources of his own mind. After 1818, his work developed a lyrical, dreamlike quality and was executed on a much smaller scale.

Old Testament subjects appear frequently in his earlier work. *The Dead Man Revived in the Tomb by Touching the Bones of the Prophet Elisha*, 1813, was painted in the style of the Sebastiano del Piombo altarpiece, *The Raising of Lazarus*, which Allston had seen in London. *Belshazzar's Feast*, painted between 1817 and 1843, was almost complete in its first form when Allston showed it to Gilbert Stuart, who recommended that some of the perspective be altered. This involved years of repainting, disrupting Allston's life, and he died before he could complete the picture.

Concurrently with *Belshazzar's Feast*, Allston painted many small landscapes. These varied in quality but at their best were full of subtlety and atmospheric richness. Although his last years were spent very quietly, Allston set new standards for American painting and he is prominent in its development.

E. P. Richardson  *Washington Allston, a Study of the Romantic Artist in America*  Chicago, *1948*

Jacob's Dream (detail) 1817
*Petworth, England*

## HIS WORKS INCLUDE

The Rising of a Thunderstorm at Sea, 1804
*Boston, Mus. Fine Arts*
The Deluge, 1804
*New York, Met. Mus.*
Belshazzar's Feast, 1817-43
*Detroit, Inst. of Arts*
Jacob's Dream, 1817
*Petworth, England*

**See also pages 154, 191**

# JOHN BACON

*A popular academic sculptor*

Born in Southwark, London, John Bacon was apprenticed at the age of 14 to a porcelain manufacturer, and this training influenced him throughout his life. He then worked as a modeler of artificial stone and in 1768 attended the Royal Academy Schools. A huge head, *Ossian*, attracted public attention and in 1769 he won the first Academy gold medal for his bas-relief, *Aeneas Escaping from Troy*.

The same year Josiah Wedgwood commissioned two reliefs from him, *The Good of the Day* and *The Good of the Night*. Bacon later produced *Mars* and *Venus*, which earned him another gold medal and the admiration of Benjamin West. This led to a commission from the Archbishop of York for a bust of George III, which was so

Sickness, 1778
*London, R. A.*

## HIS WORKS INCLUDE
Monument to the Earl of Halifax, 1771
*London, Westminster Abbey*
Monument to General Hope, 1793
*London, Westminster Abbey*
Monument to Earl Waldegrave, 1796
*Windsor, Eton College Chapel*

**See also page 203**

successful that the king ordered several copies of it, and, in 1779, obtained for Bacon the commission for the immense monument to William Pitt, Earl of Chatham, in Westminster Abbey.

Bacon was much sought after for his monumental work. He was a sculptor of great ability although at times his imagination was limited. He confounded certain critics by proving himself adept in the Classical style.

*K. A. Esdaile  English Monumental Sculpture since the Renaissance  London, 1927*

Warren Hastings, 1794
*London, N. P. G.*

## HIS WORKS INCLUDE
Monument to William Woolett, 1791
*London, Westminster Abbey*
Monument to Anna Matthews, 1793
*Chester, England, Cath.*

**See also page 206**

## THOMAS BANKS          1735-1805

*A sculptor in the Classical tradition*

Thomas Banks, born in 1735, was apprenticed to the sculptor William Barlow, and studied with Peter Scheemakers. Banks's first success came with the relief, *The Death of Epaminondas*, 1763, followed by *The Redemption of the Body of Hector*, a life-size *Prometheus*, and a design for ornamental furniture. He attended the Royal Academy Schools and received a gold medal for *The Rape of Proserpine*, 1770. In 1772 the Academy awarded him a traveling scholarship and he journeyed to Rome, returning to England in 1779. Finding commissions scarce, he then traveled to St. Petersburg and sold a marble *Cupid* to the Empress Catherine. On his return, after several commissions, he was employed by Bishop Newton's widow on a monument to her husband. Now commissions were plentiful and included *The Four Quarters of the Globe* for the Dublin Customs House. He made numerous chimney pieces, among them one for the Bank of England. His most successful monument was that to Miss Penelope Boothby, in Ashbourne Church, Derbyshire. He died in 1805.

*C. F. Bell  Annals of Thomas Banks  London, 1938*
*R. Gunnis  Dictionary of British Sculptors  London, 1957*

Raftsmen Playing Cards (detail) 1847
*St. Louis, City Art Mus.*

## GEORGE CALEB BINGHAM          1811-1879

*An American frontier painter*

George Caleb Bingham was born in Virginia in 1811, moving with his family to a frontier settlement in Missouri when he was 8. He showed an early aptitude for art, copying any engravings he could find and painting with home-made materials. Chester Harding showed him the rudiments of technique when he was traveling through Missouri, but it was 1837 before Bingham was able to study for a few months at the Pennsylvania Academy. There he learned quickly from the works of Benjamin West, Washington Allston, and Thomas Lawrence. He then painted portraits for some time in Washington and returned to Missouri about 1844.

Bingham's period in Washington gave him important connections with the American Art Union, which ensured his work a large circulation. After his return to Missouri he decided to become a painter of American "social and political characteristics" and he had the ability to seize upon the significant factors in frontier life. His paintings are simple yet luminous and subtle in style, and were used as the basis for engravings which became an important source of his income.

In 1856 Bingham went to Düsseldorf, where he came into contact with the local school of literary and sentimental narrative painting. This influenced his work unfavorably although it complied with popular taste.

Bingham returned to America in 1859. During the Civil War he enlisted with the Union Army and became involved in local politics. He was also elected professor of art in Kansas State University. He died on July 7, 1879, in Kansas City.

HIS WORKS INCLUDE

Fur Traders Descending
the Missouri, about 1845
*New York, Met. Mus.*

Raftsmen Playing Cards, 1847
*St. Louis, City Art Mus.*

Dr. Oscar F. Potter, 1848
*St. Louis, City Art Mus.*

Daniel Boone Coming through
Cumberland Gap, 1851
*St. Louis, Washington University*

**See also page 157**

---

## WILLIAM BLAKE                                      1757-1827

*A mystic, poet, painter, and engraver*

Wiliam Blake was born in Soho, London. His parents encouraged him to collect prints of the Italian masters, and in 1767 sent him to Henry Pars' drawing school. He was apprenticed to an engraver in 1772.

After his seven year term, Blake entered the Royal Academy Schools, and there formed a life-long hatred of the academic tradition represented by Sir Joshua Reynolds. He left the Academy in 1780 and soon afterwards began his friendship with Henry Fuseli. In 1782 he married, and with his wife and younger brother Robert opened a print shop. This venture failed after the death of Robert in 1787 and Blake's grief and anxiety at this time, together with the influence of his friendship with the social reformers Tom Paine and William Godwin led to the full development of his mysticism. He approved of free love, and sympathized with the actions of the French revolutionaries until the events of 1794 sickened him. Between 1794 and 1800 he lived at Lambeth, enduring a period of deep pessimism brought on by his poverty and lack of recognition.

During these years Blake earned a meager living as an engraver. Between other jobs he produced engraved editions of his own poems, the text surrounded

HIS WORKS INCLUDE

The Ancient of Days, 1794
*Manchester, England, Whitworth Art Gall.*

Newton, 1795
*London, Tate*

The Wise and Foolish Virgins,
about 1805
*London, Tate*

Satan Smiting Job, about 1825
*London, Tate*

Illustrations to the Divine Comedy,
1824-27
*London, Tate*

Copies of Blake's illuminated books are in the Library of Congress, Washington, the New York Public Library, the British Museum, London, the Fitzwilliam, Cambridge, and the Huntington, Harvard and Morgan Libraries.

**See also pages 119, 176**

Nebuchadnezzar (detail) 1795
*London, Tate*

The Wise and Foolish Virgins,
about 1805
*London, Tate*

Newton, 1795
*London, Tate*

with illustrations that he colored by hand. The process was highly original, and he experimented further in the production of prints of extraordinarily sumptuous color. In 1789 he produced *Songs of Innocence* and in 1794 *Songs of Experience*. These two sets of poems illustrate two aspects of Blake's outlook. In spite of his pessimism he was fundamentally hopeful about human nature, and all his life kept a childlike clarity of vision. This very simplicity added to the power and vehemence of his opinions and vision. He hated the effects of the Industrial Revolution in England and looked forward to the establishment of a New Jerusalem "in England's green and pleasant land." A true Romantic, he closed his eyes to the scientific discoveries of his time.

In 1800 Blake moved to Felpham in Sussex, where he worked for the poet William Hayley. The complete failure of a one-man exhibition held in 1809 at the shop once owned by his brother increased his poverty and hardship. Between 1804 and 1818 he produced an edition of his own poem *Jerusalem* with 100 engravings.

In 1818 Blake met the painter John Linnell, who commissioned a duplicate set of Blake's illustrations to the *Book of Job*, in which he was again concerned with the problem of suffering and evil. Linnell also commissioned Blake's last great work—a set of illustrations to Dante's *Divine Comedy*. These were begun in 1824, but Blake died in 1827 leaving only 7 engravings and 102 unfinished drawings. At the end of his life he acquired a circle of young admirers, including the landscape painter Samuel Palmer. The group used to gather at Linnell's house at Hampstead, and these last years seem to have been the happiest of Blake's life. It was an uncharacteristic work, a set of woodcut illustrations to Virgil's *Pastorals*, that had the greatest influence on the younger artists.

Blake was primarily a mystic, and he used the arts of poetry and painting as vehicles for his mysticism. His drawing was often deficient, but his illustrations show the power of his imagination in that they perfectly complement the written word and are at the same time of the utmost originality. Both as painter and poet, Blake was one of the great figures of the Romantic movement.

A. Blunt   *The Art of William Blake*   Oxford, 1959
A. Gilchrist   *Life of William Blake*   London, 1863; *reprint London, 1942*
G. Keynes   *William Blake's Engravings*   London, 1950
A. S. Roe   *Blake's Illustrations to the Divine Comedy*   London, 1953

---

## RICHARD PARKES BONINGTON                   1801-1828

*An English painter who lived and worked in France*

Richard Parkes Bonington was born in 1801, the son of a Nottingham drawing master. In 1817 the family settled in Calais, and the next year Bonington left home for Paris with a letter of introduction from his patron Morel to Eugène Delacroix, who was to become a close friend.

In Paris Bonington worked under Baron Gros and also studied at the Louvre.

Contrary to prevalent Parisian fashion, he preferred to sketch small landscapes in oil and watercolor. These early watercolors are remarkable for their fresh colors and apparently casual composition; the early oils are thickly impasted, but he later employed a more fluid, delicate technique. In 1821 Bonington made his first sketching tour to collect material to be worked up into finished pictures. In 1824 he won a gold medal at the Paris Salon, being one of a group of English artists, including John Constable, to arouse great interest in Paris that year.

The next year Bonington spent the summer in England with Delacroix. In 1826 he went to Italy, where he was particularly impressed by Veronese's color and Canaletto's technique, and indeed by the Venetians generally. From 1825 he also produced historical paintings, influenced by the Venetians, Watteau, and Delacroix.

In the summer of 1827 Bonington was once more in England, earning considerable sums from English engravers, but he had already contracted the pulmonary tuberculosis that in 1828 caused his death. Although his life was short, Bonington introduced into France the idea of painting directly from nature, and his work had a great influence, particularly on the Barbizon School.

*A. Dubuisson  R. P. Bonington, his Life and Work* (translated by C. E. Hughes)  *London, 1924*
*A. Shirley  Bonington  London, 1940*

Self-portrait
*London, N. P. G.*

Place du Molard, Geneva (detail) 1826
*London, V. and A.*

A Mountain Landscape, 1826
*London, Tate*

HIS WORKS INCLUDE

Scene on the French Coast, about 1827
*Oxford, Ashmolean*
Le Parterre d'Eau, Versailles, 1826
*Paris, Louvre*
Henri IV and the Spanish Ambassador, 1827
*London, Wallace Coll.*
The Column of St. Mark, Venice, 1828
*London, N. G.*

**See also page 136**

---

# FORD MADOX BROWN                               1821-1893

*An eminent painter of the mid-19th century*

Ford Madox Brown was born in Calais in 1821 and at the age of 14 was taken by his father to study art at Bruges Academy. In 1840 Brown settled in Paris, where he studied life drawing and copied the old masters, particularly Rembrandt. During these years he painted romantic historical subjects and portraits.

Brown went to Rome in 1845 and there met the German Nazarene painters Johann Friedrich Overbeck and Peter von Cornelius, who wished to revive the

HIS WORKS INCLUDE

Chaucer at the Court of Edward III, 1845-51
*Sydney, Australia, N. G.*
An English Autumn Afternoon, 1852-54
*Birmingham, England, City Art Gall.*
The Last of England, 1855
*Birmingham, England, City Art Gall.*
Work, 1852-65
*Manchester, England, City Art Gall.*

**See also page 143**

DANTE GABRIEL ROSSETTI
Portrait of Ford Madox Brown
(detail) 1852
*London, N. P. G.*

Jesus Washing Peter's Feet,
about 1856
*London, Tate*

HIS WORKS INCLUDE

Monument to Abraham Cowley,
after 1667
*London, Westminster Abbey*

Lord Mordaunt, 1675
*Fulham, London, Parish Church*

Monument to William Ashburnham
and His Wife, 1675
*London, Westminster Abbey*

Monument to Elizabeth,
Lady Myddleton, 1676
*Chirck, England, Parish Church*

**See also page 196**

spirit of medieval art, and he went to England much influenced by their ideas. In 1848 Dante Gabriel Rossetti became his pupil for a few weeks, but Brown was in fact more influenced by the Pre-Raphaelite Brotherhood than it was by him. He emulated in *Jesus Washing Peter's Feet* the naturalism of Millais' painting.

Brown's strong radical opinions were expressed in *The Last of England*, 1855, painted to draw attention to the mass emigration of the mid-19th century, and in *Work*, painted out of doors in Hampstead between 1852 and 1865. These were his two masterpieces, simple and monumental in style, and it was unfortunate that Rossetti's influence in the early 1860's caused him to change his style and concentrate on medieval themes, alternating his painting with book illustrations and designs for furniture and stained glass. Between 1878 and his death in 1893 Brown painted twelve large frescoes for Manchester Town Hall.

Brown was never recognized in his lifetime to the extent that he deserved. The critic and philosopher John Ruskin ignored him and his pictures were so badly hung at the Academy that he refused to show them there after 1855. In spite of his disconcerting changes of style and his erratic color sense, he avoided the worst excesses of Victorian taste, perhaps because of his sardonic sense of humor. He remains one of the most interesting and attractive figures of the period.

*F. M. Hueffer Ford Madox Brown London, 1896*
*R. Ironside and J. Gere Pre-Raphaelite Painters London, 1948*

## JOHN BUSHNELL died 1701

*A 17th-century monumental sculptor*

John Bushnell was apprenticed to Thomas Burman, an able sculptor. He did not complete his full term, and owing to matrimonial difficulties fled to Rome. There he studied seriously. After much traveling around Europe he eventually settled in Venice, where he worked on a large monument commemorating Alvise Mocenigo in the Church of S. Lazzaro dei Mendicanti. After 20 years abroad Bushnell was persuaded to seek the patronage of Charles II in England. He was well received by the king and commissioned in 1670 to make statues of Charles and his queen for Temple Bar. The following year he worked on statues intended for the Royal Exchange but, discovering that another sculptor had also been commissioned, he left his own work unfinished. He had become increasingly arrogant since his return to England and because of his Italian reputation expected preferential treatment. He went to extreme lengths to prove his skill, including the building of a huge replica of the Trojan Horse. Bushnell made many monuments, including a large Baroque group of 1675 to commemorate William Ashburnham and his wife, and a monument in Westminster Abbey. He began to build a house for himself near Hyde Park, but in 1701 died before its completion.

*M. Whinney and O. Millar English Art 1625-1714 Oxford, 1957*

# SIR FRANCIS CHANTREY                    1781-1841

*A celebrated sculptor of statues and portrait busts*

Francis Chantrey was born in 1781. He was apprenticed to a carver and gilder of Sheffield, and the mezzotint engraver Raphael Smith gave him drawing lessons. He wanted a painting career, and to obtain money to go to London he did portraits of the local inhabitants. In London he was employed as a woodcarver, and after a visit to Ireland, where he was seriously ill, again turned to portrait painting and began to make figures in clay. Commissions materialized, and in 1811 he exhibited a bust at the Royal Academy and was suddenly much in demand. His most successful monument was that to commemorate Marianne Johnes, which was placed in Hafod Church but destroyed by fire in 1932.

In 1814 Chantrey traveled to Paris, and in 1819 to Rome. He visited the studios of Antonio Canova and Bertel Thorwaldsen. On his return to England he set up a foundry to cast his bronze statues. His work was varied and included reliefs and busts, as well as the Minerva seal for the Athenaeum Club. He was knighted in 1835 by William IV.

G. Jones  *Sir Francis Chantrey*  *London, 1849*
T. S. R. Boase  *English Art, 1800-1870*  *Oxford, 1959*

Robert Southey (detail) 1832
*London, N. P. G.*

HIS WORKS INCLUDE

Monument to the Children of the Rev. W. Robinson, 1812
*Lichfield, England, Cath.*

Sir Robert Gillespie, 1816
*London, St. Paul's Cath.*

Monument to Richard Brinsley Sheridan, 1816
*London, Westminster Abbey*

**See also page 207**

---

# CAIUS GABRIEL CIBBER                    1630-1700

*Sculptor to William III*

Caius Gabriel Cibber was born in 1630 in Denmark, where his father was employed as a cabinetmaker at the Danish court. When he was about 17, Cibber traveled to Italy, where he stayed for several years. He then spent some time in the Netherlands, and in 1660 he went to England. There he found work with John Stone, whose father Nicholas had been master mason to Charles I.

Cibber began to work on his own in 1667, but he was incapable of organizing his finances. Thus it was that while he was carving reliefs for the base of The Monument in London, he was arrested for debt and had to return to the prison each night. Between 1687 and 1690 Cibber worked at Chatsworth, where he made garden decorations, the chapel altar, and various statues. In 1694 he began the Danish Church in Wellclose Square, demolished in 1869, which was paid for by Christian IV of Denmark. Cibber himself was buried there. In 1693 he was appointed sculptor to William III. He executed various monuments, including one to Thomas Sackville, one of his finest works, and two for the Earl of Rutland. His best-known pieces, inspired by Michelangelo's Medici tombs, are the statues of *Melancholy* and *Raving Madness* done for Bedlam Hospital.

H. Faber  *C. G. Cibber*  *Oxford, 1926*

Raving Madness (detail) 1680
*London, Guildhall Mus.*

HIS WORKS INCLUDE

Reliefs for the Monument, 1673
*London*

Melancholy and Raving Madness, 1680
*London, Guildhall Mus.*

Boy Playing Bagpipes, about 1680
*London, V. and A.*

Faith, Hope, and Charity, 1695
*Copenhagen, Ny-Carleberg Glyptothek*

**See also page 198**

# THOMAS COLE

1801-1848

*An American painter of landscapes and academic visions*

The Architect's Dream (detail) 1840
*Toledo, Ohio, Mus. of Art*

Thomas Cole was born in England in 1801. He was taken to America as a child, his family settling in the frontier region of Ohio. He became a virtually self-taught painter. He traveled for some time visiting both Philadelphia and New York, and although he settled in Catskill, a village on the Hudson River, in 1826, he used to wander on foot through the northeastern states, making sketches wherever he went. He used these as a basis for paintings in the winter when he remained in his studio.

Cole's work was immediately successful. His mixture of realism and a subjective mood, due partly to his method of work, appealed to his contemporaries. In 1829 he went to Europe, spending three years in England and Italy. In 1841 he returned to Italy, where he stayed until 1842. His visits to Europe made a great impact on him, and after his return Cole was haunted by the European scenery and its historical traditions. His attitude to painting was primarily a literary one, which was in keeping with the sentiment of his times. He was sympathetic to the Romantic school of painting, and tried to express his own feelings and moods in his work.

After 1832 Cole produced a series of allegories based on the theme of the passage of time, which were commissioned by various patrons among the intellectual circle of his day. Engravings were made of the paintings, such as *Past*, *Present*, and the four scenes of *The Voyage of Life*. They were immensely popular all over America but were spoiled by over-elaboration and triteness. Cole's painting epitomized the current sentimentality. His most striking work was *The Architect's Dream*, 1840, a heavily detailed canvas expressing his conception of life as a dream. His best work, for example *The Roman Campagna* and *An Evening in Arcady*, was done after his second visit to Italy.

HIS WORKS INCLUDE

The Oxbow of the Connecticut, 1836
*New York, Met. Mus.*

In the Catskills, 1837
*New York, Met. Mus.*

The Architect's Dream, 1840
*Toledo, Ohio, Mus. of Art.*

The Roman Campagna, 1843
*Hartford, Conn., Wadsworth Atheneum*

**See also page 155**

*E. I. Seaver   Thomas Cole   Wadsworth Atheneum, 1949*

---

# MAXIMILIAN COLT

died after 1645

*A monumental sculptor*

Maximilian Colt was the son of Maximilian Poutrain, otherwise Colt, who lived in St. Bartholomew's Close, in London. Nothing is known of the dates of his birth or death, but in his own time Colt appears to have been well known as a monumental sculptor. He was responsible for the monument to Queen Elizabeth I in Westminster Abbey. During the reign of Charles I he was in the service of the crown, for there is an entry to that effect in the office book of the Board of Works, dated 1633. Colt had two sons, one of whom appears to have been a stonecutter.

HIS WORKS INCLUDE

Monument to Queen Elizabeth I, about 1606
*London, Westminster Abbey*

Tomb of the artist's daughter Abigail, about 1629
*London, St. Bartholomew's Hospital*

**See also pages 194, 195**

*K. A. Esdaile   English Church Monuments, 1510-1840   London, 1956*

# JOHN CONSTABLE

*A major landscape painter of the 19th century*

John Constable was fortunate enough to be born the son of a Suffolk miller, who owned windmills at East Bergholt and watermills at Flatford and Dedham. Constable was to say of the surrounding countryside: "These scenes made me a painter."

By 1796 Constable was producing drawings for J. T. Smith, a topographical draftsman, writer, and exponent of the rustic taste in picturesque landscape. But Constable was not a probationer of the Royal Academy Schools until he was 23, and it was 1800 before he was admitted as a student. Influences on him at this stage were the 17th-century Dutch painters, the French landscape artist Gaspard Poussin, and Richard Wilson, whose works he copied. He was also strongly influenced by the landscapes of Thomas Gainsborough; he said: "I fancy I see Gainsborough in every hedge and hollow tree." Sir George Beaumont befriended him and allowed him to copy works in his collection. But the works of other painters were to become ever less important to Constable than nature itself. In 1802 he declared that he was "tired of running after pictures and seeking the truth at second hand," and that he believed in "laborious studies from nature."

In his early years he painted a number of portraits. In 1816 he married, despite bitter opposition from his bride's family, and after this date he painted little but landscapes. His chief works during the years between 1810 and 1820 were landscapes based on vivid, luminous sketches, such as *Weymouth Bay*. From 1820 on-

Self-portrait
*London, N. P. G.*

The Bridge at Gillingham, 1823
*London, Tate*

Maria Bicknell, later Mrs. John Constable, 1816
*London, Tate*

The Valley Farm, Willy Lott's House,
about 1835
*London, Tate*

## HIS WORKS INCLUDE

Wivenhoe Park, Essex, 1817
*Washington, D. C., N. G.*
The White Horse, 1819
*New York, Frick Coll.*
The Hay-Wain, 1821
*London, N. G.*
Salisbury Cathedral from
the Bishop's Garden, 1823
*London, V. and A.*
The Cornfield, 1826
*London, N. G.*
The Leaping Horse, 1825
*London, R. A.*

**See also pages 129, 130, 131, 175**

The Cornfield, 1826
*London, N. G.*

wards his finished paintings became more elaborate. Clouds had always been an intrinsic part of his composition, but now they became even more important, showing the influence on his style of Turner and of Rubens' painting *The Château of Steen*, which he studied at length in 1823.

These more elaborate pictures of the 1820's—which include *The Hay-Wain* and the view, *Salisbury Cathedral from the Bishop's Garden*—were produced by a more complex method. First Constable painted a study of his subject in oils in the open air. Then came a process of reconsideration and arrangement, and finally a sketch was freely painted on to canvas on the scale of the finished work. *The Hay-Wain* and *View on the Stour*, 1821, were shown at the Paris Salon of 1824. There they were a huge success, and Constable was awarded a gold medal. His work had considerable influence on the Barbizon School in France, and on the Romantic painter Eugène Delacroix.

In 1828 Constable's financial difficulties were alleviated by a legacy from his wife's father. His wife also died in that year. Constable's last works have an air of serenity, although he was far from being placid, suffering acutely from attacks made on him in the press. When he was finally made a member of the Royal Academy in 1829, the honor had been too long delayed to give him any satisfaction. He died in 1837, but the full scope of his genius was not revealed to the public until his sketches were bequeathed to the Victoria and Albert Museum by his daughter in 1888.

*C. R. Leslie   Memoirs of the Life of John Constable, ed A. Shirley   London, 1937*
*K. Badt   John Constable's Clouds   London, 1950*
*R. B. Beckett   John Constable and the Fishers   London, 1952*
*G. Reynolds   Catalogue of the Constable Collection   Victoria and Albert Museum, London, 1960*

Weymouth Bay (unfinished) 1816
*London, N. G.*

# SAMUEL COOPER                    1609-1672

*A popular miniaturist*

Samuel Cooper was born in 1609 and died in London aged 63. He first worked
with his uncle John Hoskins, limner to Charles I, and then traveled extensively,
establishing an international reputation. During the 1640's he painted both roya-
lists and parliamentarians and, after Sir Anthony van Dyck, was the most sought-
after painter of his day.

Cooper remained in London during the Commonwealth and continued to
prosper, painting portraits of Cromwell and his associates. After the restoration
of the monarchy in 1660 he was appointed limner to Charles II. Compared with
Sir Peter Lely, first painter to the king, Cooper produced better work where the
subject called for acute observation and refined execution. He commanded much
the same fee as Lely and his work was "held in the highest degree of estimation,
both in and out the Kingdom." Not only did his work please the 17th-century
taste for ingenuity, but the skill and understanding with which he portrayed his
sitters gave his work a value beyond mere fashion.

*B. S. Long   British Miniatures   London, 1929*
*G. Reynolds   English Portrait Miniatures   London, 1952*

The Rev. Mr. Stairsmore, 1657
*Cambridge, Fitzwm.*

**HIS WORKS INCLUDE**

Catherine of Braganza
*Windsor, Royal Coll.*
Oliver Cromwell, 1657
*Drumlanrig, coll. Duke of Buccleuch*

**See also page 90**

---

# JOHN SINGLETON COPLEY            1738-1815

*An American-born painter who worked in London*

John Singleton Copley was born in Boston in 1738. His stepfather, an engraver,
may have given the boy some training, but Copley was largely self-taught. He had
great natural talent, and by the time he was 25 had evolved a style of uncompromising realism ideally suited to the tastes of his New England clientèle. His direct
and distinguished portraits ensured him a comfortable living.

In 1766 he sent a portrait of his half brother to the exhibition of the Society of
Artists in London, and Benjamin West and Sir Joshua Reynolds both wrote to
him to encourage him to visit Europe. In 1769 he married Susanna Clark, the
daughter of a rich Boston merchant. The political situation of the first years of
the 1770's made him decide to leave America, and in 1774 he arrived in London,
where he was greeted by West and Reynolds. After a visit to France and Italy, he
returned to London and was joined by his family.

By this time Copley was painting historical compositions as well as portraits.
In 1778 he exhibited *Watson and the Shark* at the Royal Academy, and was immediately successful. West's painting *The Death of Wolfe* had established contemporary history as an acceptable subject, but *Watson and the Shark* was a pioneer work
in that it was romantic and exciting rather than serious. His paintings of succeeding years, *The Death of Chatham*, exhibited in 1781, and *The Death of Major Pierson*,

GILBERT STUART
Portrait of John Singleton Copley
*London, N. P. G.*

were so large that they had to be shown privately. Copley made a fortune, but antagonized the Royal Academy, which expected him to show the works at its exhibitions.

During the 1780's Copley continued to paint contemporary scenes and some historical events, such as *Charles I Demanding the Surrender of the Five Members*. These works contained much direct portraiture, and Copley turned once more to the painting of portraits as such. Now his portrait style was remodeled along the lines of George Romney and John Hoppner. At first he was successful, but after 1790 his fortunes declined. In 1799 his painting of *Admiral Duncan's Victory at Camperdown* was ignored, and his enormous *Knatchbull Family* of 1803 met with ridicule.

From 1800 both Copley's health and his work deteriorated. He was harassed by lawsuits with engravers, and he nursed a pathological envy of West, who had once been his friend. He died in 1815, having made, however, a significant contribution to the development of the Romantic movement in England.

*J. T. Flexner J. S. Copley Boston, 1948*

The Death of Chatham, about 1779
*London, Tate*

# JOHN SELL COTMAN 1782-1842

*A leading member of the Norwich School*

John Sell Cotman was the son of a Norwich tradesman. In 1798 he went to London to train as an artist, but he had no formal teaching. Instead he colored prints, and worked for Dr. Thomas Monro, a philanthropic amateur draftsman.

In 1800 Cotman went to Wales with Thomas Girtin, the first of many journeys throughout England and Wales. By 1805 he had broken away from Girtin's influence and found his own personal style. His method was to make a light sketch in pencil, tint it with color washes, and then to pick out salient details with a reed pen.

Cotman returned to Norwich in 1806. He became a member of the Norwich Society of Artists, and contributed to their annual exhibitions, becoming president in 1811. By then he frequently painted in oils, but these paintings were cruder than his early works and he had little success with them. In 1812 he became drawing master to the family of Dawson Turner, a wealthy banker and antiquarian in Yarmouth. The two men were friends, sharing a love of old buildings, and in 1818 Cotman published a book, *Etchings Illustrative of the Architectural Antiquities of Norfolk*, with sixty illustrations. This was followed by *Sepulchral Brasses in Norfolk*.

In 1817, 1818 and 1820 Cotman toured Normandy with Turner, and in 1823 returned to Norwich with his wife and five children. He continued to teach. By then his work in oils had improved, although his watercolors, becoming more mannered, had lost the charm of his early works. In 1834 he was appointed professor of drawing at King's College in London, and this to a certain extent relieved his financial difficulties. His last years were dogged by ill-health and depression.

*A. P. Oppé   The Watercolor Drawings of John Sell Cotman   London, 1923*
*S. D. Kitson   John Sell Cotman   London, 1937*

The Drop Gate, about 1826
*London, Tate*

# DAVID COX                                    1783-1859

*A landscape painter in watercolor*

David Cox's father was a Birmingham blacksmith, and the painter received little formal training in art. He was apprenticed to a toymaker, and later to a painter of miniature portraits; meanwhile he took lessons from a local painter, Joseph Barber. He also worked as a scene painter in the Birmingham theater.

In 1804 Cox went to London and in 1805 exhibited at the Royal Academy for the first time, although most of his work was to be shown at the Watercolor Society's annual exhibitions. In 1808 he married and moved to Dulwich, then a quiet village just outside London, where he established a reputation as a watercolor painter and teacher. He also wrote a number of popular instructive works. Leaving London in 1814 for Hertford, he continued to work as a teacher and topographical artist. He visited London regularly, and each summer made extensive sketching tours in Yorkshire, Derbyshire, and Wales. He traveled abroad three times, to Holland, Belgium and France, and in 1827 returned to live in London.

Cox's reputation was made with small, highly colored and intricate watercolors of rustic scenes. In 1836, however, he discovered that a rough, slightly tinted wrapping paper gave a good effect when painted with a fully charged brush. The freer paintings of more rugged scenery that resulted mark his mature period, but his broad effects are sometimes spoiled by a forced appearance.

From 1840 Cox took lessons in oils, and became extremely able in this medium. In 1841 he retired to Harborne, near Birmingham, spending his summers in North Wales. The works of his last years, particularly the oils, are often repetitions of earlier watercolors.

*Trenchard Cox   David Cox   London, 1947*

W. BOXALL
Portrait of David Cox
(detail) 1857
*London, N. P. G.*

## HIS WORKS INCLUDE

The Night Train
*Birmingham, England, City Art Gall.*

Asking the Way, about 1850
*Birmingham, England, City Art Gall.*

The principal collections of Cox's oils and watercolors are to be found in London, the British Museum and the Victoria and Albert Museum, and the City Museum and Art Gallery, Birmingham.

**See also page 133**

# ALEXANDER COZENS

about 1717-1786

*A watercolor painter*

Landscape
*London, B. M.*

Alexander Cozens was born in Russia about 1717, but by 1742 he had settled in England. He visited Italy in 1746 and two years later was again on the continent. He made many landscape sketches, mostly in pen and wash, treated with great spontaneity.

He held several important teaching posts, and in 1781 was drawing instructor to the young sons of George III. From 1760-81 he exhibited at the Society of Artists and at the Royal Academy. His work contained great vivacity within the scope to which he limited himself. He worked mainly in monochrome, but achieved great breadth and luminosity. Constable learned much from his remarkable sky studies, and one of Cozens' most celebrated achievements was the invention of the "blot" landscape, which was evolved to encourage his pupils to compose more freely. He suggested that they should brush in some general form, and then work out a composition from the suggested shapes. Although Cozens never achieved the fame of his son, John Robert Cozens, he is now accepted with Paul Sandby as one of the two greatest early 18th-century watercolorists.

*A. P. Oppé Alexander and John Robert Cozens London, 1952*

---

# JOHN ROBERT COZENS

1752-1797

*A painter of Romantic landscapes*

Little is known of Cozens' early life, except that he was born in London, and that Alexander Cozens was his father. All his known works are landscapes.

In 1776 Cozens exhibited an oil painting, *Hannibal Crossing the Alps*, at the Royal Academy, but this work is now lost. Almost all his work is based on two Italian journeys, the first undertaken in 1776 when he traveled through Switzerland and into Italy as far as Florence. He was in Rome in 1778, and his style was modified by his contact with the Swiss watercolorists. At first his color range was small, varying from greys to blue-greens, but his later works, particularly those of his second journey to Italy in 1782, have a richer and more varied palette and a more strongly Romantic sense of atmosphere. Cozens "composed" his landscapes, altering what he saw to make it more poetic. He often repeated works and in 1789 painted *View of Elba* from a sketch by his father. English scenery did not stimulate his imagination in the same way.

In 1793 Cozens' mind gave way. He died in 1797, having founded a new style of landscape painting in England. John Constable declared, with more generosity than truth, but nevertheless acknowledging a debt, that Cozens was "the greatest genius that ever touched landscape."

*A. P. Oppé Alexander and John Robert Cozens London, 1952*

# JOHN CROME                                        1768-1821

*A landscape painter who founded the Norwich School*

John Crome began life as an errand boy in Norwich, but following his natural inclination he apprenticed himself to a signmaker. He copied the works of Gainsborough and various 17th-century Dutch landscapes in the collection of a local collector, Thomas Harvey. Crome's first known oil sketch is of 1790.

When he was in his early twenties Crome met two professional portrait painters, William Beechey and John Opie, who provided a view of art that had been lacking in his provincial experience. By 1798 he was established as a drawing master to local families, one of which took him on a visit to the Lake District and Wales. He later became an art master at Norwich Grammar School, and was the first teacher of painting to take his pupils out into the open air. In 1803 he became a founder member of the Norwich Society of Artists, and its president in 1808.

As Crome did not date his works and the subjects are all similar, being scenes of the Norfolk countryside, it is not easy to trace any definite line of development. The chief influences on him were those of Richard Wilson and Thomas Gainsborough. The *Slate Quarries*, 1805, is a typical work, showing in its broad and simple forms and clear light a straightforward, natural feeling for color. In 1814 Crome traveled to France to see the Napoleonic collections, but it was the new landscapes of his journey that stimulated his imagination. They affected his later works, such as *The Poringland Oak* and *Mousehold Heath* with an increased breadth and serenity. Crome's attitude to the often homely scenes that he painted is shown in his advice to his son, "John, my boy, paint, but paint for fame, and if your subject be only a pigsty, dignify it."

*L. Binyon   John Crome and John Sell Cotman   London, 1897*
*C. H. Collins Baker   Crome   London, 1921*

M. B. MURPHY
Portrait of John Crome
*London, N. P. G.*

### HIS WORKS INCLUDE

Slate Quarries, 1805
*London, Tate*

Moonrise on the Yare, about 1816
*London, Tate*

View on Mousehold Heath, about 1812
*London, V. and A.*

The Poringland Oak, about 1818
*London, N. G.*

**See also page 122**

---

# ARTHUR DEVIS                                        1711-1787

*A painter of conversation pièces*

Arthur Devis was a painter of portraits and conversation pieces for those who preferred his provincial art to that of the more skilled and fashionable masters, William Hogarth, Johann Zoffany and the young Thomas Gainsborough. Devis learned his trade from Peter Tillemans, a topographical painter from Antwerp. During the first years of his career Devis traveled round England painting small-scale portraits of country landowners posing in their fields and gardens. Later, he made his headquarters in London, and from 1761 to 1790 he showed works at the exhibitions of the Society of Artists. He was elected president in 1768, but the importance of the Society had already been overshadowed by that of the newly founded Royal Academy. By the 1770's conversation pieces were a waning fashion,

Gentleman at a Reading Desk
(detail) 1761
*Manchester, England, City Art Gall.*

and, for the work available, Zoffany was the most popular master. Devis spent his last years experimenting with painting on glass and working as a restorer.

Devis's work, though naïve, with its clear colors and widely spaced, rather wooden figures, has great charm. His style changed little throughout his life. His half brother, Anthony Devis, was a landscape painter who worked mainly in watercolor, and two of Arthur's sons painted portraits and historical subjects.

*S. H. Pavière   The Devis Family   Leigh-on-Sea, England, 1956*

**See also page 100**

HIS WORKS INCLUDE
Mr. and Mrs. William Atherton, about 1747
*Liverpool, England, Walker Art Gall.*
The Vanneck Family, 1752
*Prides Crossing, Mass., coll. Miss Helen Frick*

---

## WILLIAM DOBSON                                            1610-1646

*A portrait painter who established a sturdily independent style*

William Dobson was born in London in 1610. His master was the Flemish painter Franz Cleyn, and from him and from the Venetian pictures in the Royal Collection Dobson learned the traditions of the Venetian school. His style became almost independent of Sir Anthony van Dyck, and on van Dyck's death the field was open for Dobson.

From 1642 Dobson painted official portraits of the court in London and Oxford. The royal children and entourage are nearly all painted half length, not elegant in van Dyck's manner, but robust. The accessories, often sculptural, were intended to be relevant to the subject. Dobson's manner was especially suited to the portrayal of stern fighting men, as van Dyck's had been to the exquisite courtier.

*O. Millar   Catalogue of the William Dobson Exhibition   Tate Gallery, London, 1951*

HIS WORKS INCLUDE
John, 1st Baron Byron
*Tabley House, coll. Lt. Col. J. L. B. Leicester-Warren*
Prince Rupert with Colonels Murray and Russell
*Ombersley Court, Worcs., England, coll. Lord Sandys*
Sir William Compton
*Castle Ashby, England, coll. Marquess of Northampton*
William Dobson, Sir Charles Cotterell, and Sir Balthazar Gerbier, about 1645
*Albury, England, coll. Helen, Duchess of Northumberland*

**See also page 91**

---

## WILLIAM DYCE                                              1806-1864

*A painter, scientist and reformer*

William Dyce studied in the Academy Schools in London. Later, while studying in Rome, he met the Nazarenes, and introduced their ideas to England with his *Madonna*, 1828. He turned to scientific study, but established himself as a portrait painter in Edinburgh in 1830. A pamphlet proposing his art education reforms led to his being sent to examine state art schools abroad. In 1840 he became director of the School of Design in London but shortly after resigned. Inspired by the Nazarenes to revive fresco in England, he designed in 1846 the *Baptism of Ethelbert* for the House of Lords.

Dyce's portraits and religious subjects are his best works, but it is as teacher and theorist that he is chiefly honored. He refused the presidency of the Academy in 1850, but in 1864 became professor of the theory of fine art at King's College, London.

*J. Caw   Scottish Painting, 1620-1908   London, 1908*

HIS WORKS INCLUDE
Joash Shooting the Arrow, 1844
*Hamburg, Kunsthalle*
Pegwell Bay, Kent, about 1860
*London, Tate*
The Woman of Samaria, about 1860
*Birmingham, England, City Art Gall.*
George Herbert at Bemerton, 1861
*London, Guildhall*

**See also page 139**

# WILLIAM ETTY

1787-1849

*A painter of the English Romantic school*

William Etty was born in York the son of a miller and baker, and as a boy was apprenticed as a printer's compositor in Hull. In 1805 he left for London, determined to become a painter. From 1807 he attended the Royal Academy Schools and took lessons privately from Sir Thomas Lawrence.

Although he painted many historical and genre compositions, by far the largest proportion of his work consists of nude studies. He was one of the very few English painters to paint nudes almost exclusively, his style being derived from Titian and Rubens. In 1811 he exhibited at the Royal Academy and the British Institute two paintings, *Sappho* and *Telemachus*, now lost. In 1815 he made an extensive tour of the continent, and between 1822 and 1824 he stayed in Paris, Rome, Venice and Florence making many copies, especially of the works of Titian and Rubens. During his stay in Paris he met Eugène Delacroix, a painter with whom he had much in common.

Etty had achieved popular success in 1821 with *Cleopatra's Arrival in Cilicia*. This was an ambitious, crowded work of Baroque splendour. He followed it with *Pandora* of 1824, and in the same year, *The Combat*, a huge figure composition. He also painted and exhibited many large historical pictures, such as the *Judith and Holofernes*. In 1831 he painted *The Window in Venice*, the first of a new kind of painting, the fancy-dress composition, which showed a typical Romantic interest in medieval dress and life.

After 1834 Etty's health declined and his work deteriorated. When a large triptych, *Joan of Arc*, had been received with indifference at the Royal Academy exhibition of 1847, he retired to York, where he died in 1849.

*D. Farr William Etty London, 1958*

Self-portrait
*Manchester, England, City Art Gall.*

## HIS WORKS INCLUDE

Cleopatra's Arrival in Cilicia, 1821
*Port Sunlight, England,*
*Lady Lever Art Gall.*
The Combat, 1824
*Edinburgh, N. G. of Scotland*
Youth on the Prow and Pleasure
at the Helm, 1832
*London, Tate*
The Sirens and Ulysses, 1837
*Manchester, England, City Art Gall.*

**See also page 135**

Study of a Man in Persian Costume,
about 1834
*London, Tate*

The Bather "At the Doubtful Breeze
Alarmed," about 1848
*London, Tate*

The Lute Player, about 1833
*London, Tate*

Queen Elizabeth Confounding Juno,
Minerva and Venus, 1569
*Hampton Court, Royal Coll.*

## HIS WORKS INCLUDE

Turk on Horseback, 1549
*Brocklesby Park, coll. Earl of Yarborough*

Sir John Luttrell, 1550
*Dunster Castle, coll. G. F. Luttrell*

Queen Elizabeth Confounding Juno,
Minerva, and Venus, 1569
*Hampton Court, Royal Coll.*

**See also page 86**

## HANS EWORTH                    active 1545 or 1549-1574

*A Fleming who worked at the court of Elizabeth I*

Hans Eworth was born in Antwerp and came to London in 1545 or 1549, staying until 1574. There are about 30 signed and dated works of this period. *Turk on Horseback*, 1549, like his later works, is painted in a fastidious style with a wealth of detail. His early portraits, for example *Sir John Luttrell*, 1550, are set in landscapes rich in allegory and appropriate incident.

By 1554, Eworth was painting Queen Mary and other court figures. His work became more sober in the Holbein manner, but lacking Holbein's robustness. His last works show the emphasis on costume and furniture fashionable in Elizabeth I's court. The 25-inch-high double portrait of *Lord Darnley and his Brother*, 1563, is in this manner, the type of large miniature scale being well suited to the tastes and the pockets of the country gentry. Eworth's most remarkable work is a picture of *Queen Elizabeth Confounding Juno, Minerva, and Venus*, proof that Eworth had learned the hyperbolical flattery elegantly expressed that was always acceptable to Queen Elizabeth.

*E. K. Waterhouse   Painting in Britain, 1530-1790   London, 1953*

---

## HIS WORKS INCLUDE

General Samuel Waldo, about 1748
*Brunswick, Me., Mus., Bowdoin Coll.*

Pamela Andrews, about 1745
*Providence, Rhode Island, Mus. of Art*

**See also page 147**

## ROBERT FEKE                    about 1710 - about 1750

*An early American portraitist*

Robert Feke was born at Oyster Bay, Long Island. Little is known of his early life, other than he was at some time a sailor. His first work was a large portrait composition of Isaac Royall's family, painted in Boston. It is the product of an inexperienced hand, but it is bold and clear, and influenced in style by John Smibert.

Feke worked in Philadelphia and Newport, and between 1741 and 1750 he painted at least 70 portraits. He owed much to the Baroque influences introduced by Smibert, and his early work particularly was poetic and spontaneous. He was not an analytical portraitist, but his work was strong and dignified, if sometimes slightly stiff. After 1750 he disappeared; it is said that he died in the West Indies.

*H. W. Foote   Robert Feke, Colonial Portrait Painter   Harvard, 1930*

---

## HIS WORKS INCLUDE

Bust of Pasquale di Paoli, 1807
*London, Westminster Abbey*

Monument to Viscount Nelson, 1809
*London, St. Paul's Cath.*

Robert Burns, 1822
*Edinburgh, N. P. G.*

**See also page 205**

## JOHN FLAXMAN                    1755-1826

*A Neoclassic sculptor of European reputation*

John Flaxman was the son of a modeler who worked for Josiah Wedgwood. He began to model at an early age and his ability soon attracted the attention of friends such as George Romney.

Flaxman gained prizes at the Society of Arts and in 1770 won a gold medal for a statue of David Garrick. He attended the Academy Schools and in 1775 began to model and design for Wedgwood. Among the subjects of his cameo portraits were Sarah Siddons and Sir Joshua Reynolds. Flaxman also assisted in the decoration of Etruria Hall, and in 1787 Wedgwood sent him to Rome. During his seven year stay Flaxman began to form a reputation as an illustrator. He was commissioned to illustrate the poems of Homer and Dante, and the tragedies of Aeschylus. Many of these were engraved in Rome in 1793 and became famous throughout Europe. He returned to England in 1794, having been elected to the academies of Florence and Carrara.

On his return to London, Flaxman worked mainly on monumental sculpture. He exhibited with the Academy from 1787 and was appointed professor of sculpture by the Academy in 1810.

W. G. Constable  *J. Flaxman*  London, 1927
T. S. R. Boase  *English Art, 1800-1870*  Oxford, 1959

Self-portrait, 1778
*London, V. and A.*

JOHNNES FLAXMAN

---

## GERLACH FLICKE  died 1558

*A foreign painter who worked at the court of Henry VIII*

Gerlach Flicke was a German who lived in London from about 1545. In 1547 he signed and dated a portrait of an unknown nobleman, traditionally identified with the 13th Lord Grey de Wilton. This work is in the style of his native Westphalia, but the signed portrait of Archbishop Thomas Cranmer, painted within the year, already shows the influence of the Holbeinesque style of Henry VIII's court. Flicke's work for Henry VIII shows an increasing tendency to Italianate motifs, together with backgrounds made up of the architecture of the period.

The only other work certainly by Flicke is an uncharacteristic diptych, painted in about 1554. This shows his own portrait as a prisoner in Strangeways jail with that of a fellow prisoner. Flicke died in 1558, a resident of Cripplegate in London.

**HIS WORKS INCLUDE**
An Unknown Nobleman, 1547
*Edinburgh, N. G. of Scotland*
Archbishop Cranmer, 1547
*London, N. P. G.*
Sir William Carew,
*Edinburgh, N. G. of Scotland*

**See also page 85**

---

## WILLIAM POWELL FRITH  1819-1909

*A painter of the Victorian scene*

William Powell Frith was the son of a Yorkshire publican who encouraged him to take drawing seriously. In 1835, when he was 16, Frith went to Sass's School of Art in London and there met Edward Lear. In 1837 he went to the Royal Academy Schools and the next year exhibited *A Page with a Letter* at the British Institute. For some time Frith painted historical and literary scenes, for example, *Malvolio, Cross-gartered before the Countess Olivia*. In 1842 he began the Dolly Varden series, illustrations to Dickens' *Barnaby Rudge*.

Self-portrait, 1838
*London, N. P. G.*

Derby Day (detail) 1858
*London, Tate*

HIS WORKS INCLUDE

Ramsgate Sands, 1854
*London, Royal Coll.*

The Artist's Model, 1856
*Derby, England, Mus. and Art Gall.*

Derby Day, 1858
*London, Tate*

**See also page 142**

In 1837 Frith had become one of "The Clique," a group of young men critical of fashionable academism. He was interested in the possibilities of painting contemporary life, but the difficulty of making modern clothing pictorially acceptable and the fear that such painting would be unpopular made him hesitate, and his first essay, perhaps encouraged by the Pre-Raphaelites whom he in fact despised, was not executed until 1852. *Bedtime* was followed in 1854 by *Ramsgate Sands*, an ambitious painting of contemporary life which was exhibited at the Academy and bought by Queen Victoria. The traditions of David Wilkie and William Mulready were the strongest influence in these works by Frith. In particular, he adopted Wilkie's methods of composition, with lines of small figures arranged across the canvas. In 1858 he exhibited his most famous painting, *Derby Day*, and in 1862 produced *The Railway Station*. From this time on he was engaged mainly in painting canvases depicting the life of the Victorian middle class. His work is pleasing and well painted, the compositions are more subtle than they first appear, and the canvases are full of incident. He did not succumb to an undue extent to the Victorian habit of moralizing, even in *Road to Ruin*, 1878, and *Race for Wealth*, 1880. In his last years he was out of fashion, and he died in London in 1909.

*W. P. Frith   My Autobiography and Reminiscences   London, 1888*
*G. Reynolds   Painters of the Victorian Scene   London, 1953*

The Railway Station,
completed 1862
*Egham, England, Royal
Holloway College*

---

HENRY FUSELI                                                          1741-1825

*A Swiss-born history painter of the early Romantic school*

HIS WORKS INCLUDE

The Nightmare, about 1781
*Zürich, Kunsthaus*

Falstaff in the Buck Basket, 1792
*Zürich, Kunsthaus*

Sin Pursued by Death, 1791-99
*Zürich, Kunsthaus*

**See also pages 118, 177**

Henry Fuseli was Swiss by birth. After a short and unsuccessful career as a clergyman, undertaken in deference to his father's wishes, he emigrated to England. He had studied art in Berlin for a short time in 1763, and his first years in England, which he looked upon as the home of religious and political freedom, were spent as a hack translator and illustrator. Eventually he won the notice of Sir Joshua Reynolds, who encouraged him to go to Rome in 1770. He stayed there until 1778, teaching himself by copying the works of Michelangelo.

On his return to England, Fuseli was almost immediately successful with a romantic horror picture, *The Nightmare*. This work shows the characteristic distortions of his style, particularly in the slightly erotic figure of the woman. Fuseli worked for Boydell's Shakespeare Gallery, and became a member of the Royal Academy in 1790. This encouraged him to set up a Milton Gallery of his own, but the 46 huge works illustrating *Paradise Lost* were not successful with critics or public.

In 1800 Fuseli was made professor of painting at the Academy, and in 1804 was given the position of keeper, with rooms at Somerset House. He held both posts until his death, and was a much respected teacher, renowned for his sarcasm and eccentricity. William Etty, the history painter Benjamin Robert Haydon, John Constable, and Edwin Landseer were among his pupils. In 1820 he published a volume of lectures on painting.

Fuseli's work demonstrates the horrific, heroic, and dramatic qualities of early Romanticism. About 1780 he met William Blake, and their work is in some respects similar, though Fuseli fell far short of Blake's powerful mysticism. Like many of the Romantic artists, Fuseli neglected the craft of painting, with the result that many of his works have deteriorated with time.

*J. Knowles   Life and Writings of Henry Fuseli   London, 1831*
*F. Antal   Fuseli Studies   London, 1956*

Self-portrait
London, V. and A.

---

## THOMAS GAINSBOROUGH                                    1727-1788

*A painter eminent both in landscape and portraiture*

Thomas Gainsborough was by natural inclination a painter of landscapes, but he became one of the most successful portrait painters of his day. His genius was lyrical, his portraits the essence of Rococo grace; in contrast with his rival Reynolds, he had little psychological or intellectual interest in his sitters. It is significant that while Reynolds numbered the great literary figures of the day among his friends, Gainsborough found his relaxation with musicians.

Gainsborough was the son of a once prosperous cloth-merchant of Sudbury in Suffolk. In about 1740 he was sent to London, where he had no formal academic training but worked with the French engraver Hubert Gravelot, and copied and restored Dutch 17th-century landscapes. These landscapes were the principal influence on his early works, such as *Cornard Wood*, dated 1748 but begun, he said, before he left school.

In 1746 Gainsborough married Margaret Burr, a natural daughter of the Duke of Beaufort, who brought him an annual income of £200. The young couple remained in London for four years, during which time he painted *The Charterhouse* for the Foundling Hospital, which, unlike its companions in a collection of topographical works, was a pictorial composition in its own right. In 1748 his father died, and he returned to Sudbury. In 1750 Gainsborough moved into Ipswich and in 1759 went to Bath in search of a more fashionable clientèle. By this time, small-scale portraiture was no longer in vogue, and Gainsborough's work became more sophisticated to satisfy his more sophisticated sitters. His portraits were now formal and life size, for example *Mrs. Henry Portman*, 1763. The influence of van Dyck,

Self-portrait, with his Wife and Child
*Houghton, Norfolk, coll. The Marquis of Cholmondeley*

whose work he saw in collections near Bath, led him even to dress some of his sitters in van Dyck costumes, like the one which Jonathan Buttall wears in the portrait of 1770, *The Blue Boy*. Gainsborough painted much by candlelight, delighting in the play of light and shade on silk and velvet. Most of his best portraits are of women, but probably the finest of all are those which he painted when there was no patron to be pleased, for instance the two unfinished pictures of his daughters, Mary and Margaret, and his unfinished self-portrait.

In his fifteen years at Bath Gainsborough painted few landscapes, and these, such as the *Harvest Wagon* of about 1767, are more composed than observed, richer in color than his earlier works, and show the influence of Rubens. In 1774 Gainsborough moved to London, where he lived in Pall Mall for the rest of his life. In 1768 he had been made a founder-member of the Royal Academy, and later a member of its council, but in 1773 he resigned after a quarrel over the hanging of his pictures, and he did not exhibit at the Academy again until 1777. Another quarrel led him to show his works only at private summer exhibitions in his own home for the rest of his life. Gainsborough's natural rival was Reynolds, a painter with more insight into the characters of his sitters, but with less elegance and grace. Reynolds was a knight and the head of the Academy, yet it was Gainsborough whom members of the Royal Family preferred to paint their portraits.

During the last years of his life Gainsborough turned once more to landscapes, and to rural genre subjects, such as *A Peasant Smoking at a Cottage Door, with his Family*, which Reynolds called "fancy pictures." In 1783 he visited the Lake District, where he painted mountain landscapes. He was one of the few successful

The Painter's Daughters Chasing
a Butterfly (unfinished) about 1758
*London, N. G.*

The Baillie Family, about 1784
*London, Tate*

painters of his time who never employed drapery men or other assistants. To get his vivacious effects he used long brushes and painted thinly, and as a result his works have lasted well. Gainsborough's manner was too personal and lyrical to be handed on, but his "fancy pictures" were imitated for a short while.

Delightful as Gainsborough's portraits are, it is probable that his landscapes were the more important in the development of English art, for they look forward to the landscape painters of the 19th century, especially to the greatest of them, John Constable. Gainsborough died in 1788.

*W. T. Whitley  Thomas Gainsborough  London, 1915*
*M. Woodall  Gainsborough's Landscape Drawings  London, 1939*
*E. K. Waterhouse  Gainsborough  London, 1958*

Diana and Actaeon (detail)
*London, Royal Coll.*

The Charterhouse, about 1748
*London, Coram Foundation*

View of Denham, about 1753
*London, Tate*

The Morning Walk, 1785
*London, N. G.*

## GRINLING GIBBONS

1648-1720

*A virtuoso woodcarver*

Grinling Gibbons was born in Rotterdam, where his father was a draper. When the family returned to England he was admitted to the Drapers' Company by virtue of his father's profession. He is reputed to have taken up shipcarving for a time, and then appears to have been employed to carve decorations for the playhouse called the Duke's House, in Dorset Gardens, London.

Gibbons was at this time living at Deptford near the house of the diarist John Evelyn. Evelyn recounts in his diary how he found Gibbons carving in wood a copy of Tintoretto's *Crucifixion*, which "for curiosity of handling, drawing and studious exactness, I had never before seen in all my travels." On the strength of this Evelyn took Gibbons to the court at Whitehall, and introduced him to the architect Sir Christopher Wren. Wren employed him to carve a chimneypiece at Windsor. The king, Charles II, recognized Gibbons' extraordinary ability, and appointed him master carver in wood to the crown, a post which he held until the reign of George I. Gibbons founded a workshop, and much of the carving was in fact carried out by his assistants.

Evelyn continued to befriend the carver by recommendations, and Gibbons carried out a considerable number of commissions for statues and carvings in marble. Much of his work in wood has been destroyed by fire. Among his monuments are those to Sir Richard Browne, in St. Nicholas' Church, Deptford, and to the Duke of Chandos and his wives, at St. Lawrence's Church, Whitchurch.

*M. Whinney and O. Millar   English Art, 1625-1714   Oxford, 1957*

Grinling Gibbons (detail)
after a portrait by Godfrey Kneller
*London, N. P. G.*

### HIS WORKS INCLUDE

James II, 1686
*London, Trafalgar Square*
Monument to Sir Richard Head, 1689
*Rochester, England, Cath.*
Monument to Admiral
Sir Cloudesley Shovel, 1707
*London, Westminster Abbey*
There are wooden chimneypieces by Gibbons in many of the great houses in England.

**See also page 199**

---

## I.GIBSON

## JOHN GIBSON

1790-1866

*An English sculptor who lived and worked in Rome*

John Gibson's career as a sculptor began in 1805 when, at the age of 15, he met the sculptor, F. A. Legé. Gibson copied Legé's *Head of Bacchus* and produced *Head of Mercury* in marble. He was apprenticed to a firm of Liverpool statuaries and soon executed a bas-relief and a monument to Henry Blundell, placed in Sefton Church, Lancashire, in 1813. In 1816 he exhibited at the Academy and, armed with introductions, came to London, perhaps studying under Joseph Nollekens. The next year he went to Rome to study under Antonio Canova, and was helped by the Danish sculptor, Bertel Thorwaldsen. He executed several commissions for patrons in England, including *Mars* and *Cupid* for the Duke of Devonshire.

Gibson introduced the practice of tinting marble, a device used in ancient Greece. In 1844, and again in 1850, he returned to England to make a tinted statue of Queen Victoria. The delicately colored *Tinted Venus* is his most celebrated work. He died, honored and successful, in Rome in 1866, leaving most of his money and the contents of his studio to the Royal Academy.

### HIS WORKS INCLUDE

John Philip Kemble, 1814
*London, N. P. G.*
Hylas and the Naiads, 1826
*London, Tate*

**See also page 208**

# THOMAS GIRTIN

1775-1802

*A central figure of the British watercolor school*

Thomas Girtin was born at Southwark in London, the son of a brushmaker. In 1789 he was apprenticed to Edward Dayes, a topographical painter and engraver, but before long the two of them quarreled and parted company. From 1791 to 1795 he was employed as a topographical artist by the antiquary James Moore, working up his rough sketches of castles and monasteries into a form suitable for publication. His first exhibition work was a view of Ely Cathedral.

In 1794 Girtin was employed by Dr. Thomas Monro, a philanthropic amateur draftsman who befriended many young artists. Turner, born in the same year as Girtin, worked for Dr. Monro at the same time, and generously said in later years, "If Tom Girtin had lived, I should have starved." They worked together to make copies of drawings by John Cozens, and a diary of 1798 records that "Girtin drew in outlines, and Turner washed in effects." Girtin also copied the topographical drawings of Canaletto.

In 1796 and succeeding years Girtin toured in England, Wales, and the Scottish lowlands. Although almost all his works were then simple landscapes, he still painted some topographical subjects, such as *Durham Cathedral*, 1797.

In 1800 he married the daughter of a wealthy goldsmith, and a son was born to them a year later. In 1801 also he exhibited his last painting at the Royal Academy —*Bolton Abbey* in oils, now lost. In 1801 and 1802 Girtin lived in France, because of ill health. He drew 20 views of Paris, which were engraved and published posthumously, for he died soon after his return to London. In a short life he had proved that in freedom and breadth of feeling, watercolor could be as eloquent a medium as oils.

*T. Girtin and D. Loshak   The Art of Thomas Girtin   London, 1954*

JOHN OPIE
Portrait of Thomas Girtin
*London, N. P. G.*

HIS WORKS INCLUDE

Peterborough Cathedral, 1797
*Manchester, England, Whitworth Art Gall*
The White House, Chelsea, 1800
*London, Tate*
Kirkstall Abbey, about 1801
*London, V. and A.*
La Rue St. Denis, Paris, 1801
*Coll. Sir Edmond Bacon*

**See also page 123**

---

# CHRISTOPHER HEWETSON

1739-1799

*An Irish sculptor*

Christopher Hewetson was born in Ireland in 1739. He showed an exceptional talent for sculpture, and friends paid for him to study in Rome. During his stay there he began, in 1772, an imposing monument, *Doctor Baldwin*. This was completed in 1781, and was set up in the Examination Hall of Trinity College, Dublin, in 1784. For this work he received a handsome payment. Between 1786 and 1790, Hewetson exhibited at the Royal Academy, mainly showing busts of notable contemporaries. He died in Rome in 1799.

*T. Hodgkinson   Christopher Hewetson, an Irish Sculptor in Rome*
*The Walpole Society, Vol. XXXIV, Glasgow, 1958*

HIS WORKS INCLUDE

The Duke of Gloucester, 1772
*Windsor, Royal Coll.*
Pope Clement XIV, 1776
*London, V. and A.*
Cardinal Rezzonico, after 1783
*Rome, S. Nicola in Carcere*

**See also page 204**

Mr. Oldham and his Guests, 1740-50
*London, Tate*

## JOSEPH HIGHMORE                    1692-1780

*A painter of portraits and scenes from literature*

Joseph Highmore, a contemporary of William Hogarth, was born in London, where he trained to be a lawyer. For ten years he spent his leisure hours at Kneller's Academy, and when his clerkship expired in 1714 became a professional painter. Few of his early works are known, the earliest being a portrait of 1721 and a portrait etching of 1723. He particularly admired the paintings of Rubens he had seen on a visit to Düsseldorf and Antwerp, and his portraits became more full-blooded and genial in the style of Hogarth's *Captain Coram*. A portrait of Samuel Richardson in 1750 typifies his style in portraiture.

Highmore achieved his greatest success with a series of narrative paintings illustrating Richardson's novel *Pamela*. This work also resembles Hogarth's but lacks the satirical element. Predominant is a Rococo flavor showing the influence of the engraver Hubert Gravelot.

### HIS WORKS INCLUDE

The Pamela Series, about 1744
*London, Tate; Cambridge, Fitzwm;
Melbourne, Australia, N. G.*
Hagar and Ishmael, 1746
*London, Coram Foundation*
Mr. Oldham and his Guests, 1740-50
*London, Tate*
Samuel Richardson
*London, N. P. G.*

**See also page 95**

Gentleman in a Brown Velvet
Coat (detail) 1747
*London, Tate*

## NICHOLAS HILLIARD                   1547-1619

*The greatest of English miniaturists*

Nicholas Hilliard was born into a family of goldsmiths in Exeter. He was apprenticed to a goldsmith and jeweler, and by the age of 13 he had produced at least two of the miniature portraits that were at that time looked upon as jewels, to be worn about the person as brooches or lockets.

By 1570 Hilliard had become a member of the Goldsmiths' Company in London, and in 1576 he married Alice Brandon, the daughter of the Chamberlain of the City of London. In about 1577 Hilliard visited France, where he met the poet Ronsard and received commissions from the Duke of Alençon.

It is not known exactly when Hilliard was appointed limner and goldsmith to Elizabeth I, but his earliest known portrait of her, rather stiffly and quaintly painted, dates from the 1560's. Hilliard was obviously well received at court; his

### HIS WORKS INCLUDE

The Artist's Wife, 1578
*London, V. and A.*
Portrait of a Man against
a Background of Flames, about 1595
*London, V. and A.*
There are several portraits of Queen Elizabeth I, of which two are in London, V. and A., and one in Cambridge, Fitzwilliam. The others are in private collections.

**See also pages 87, 161**

fashionable talent and handsome person ensured this. In his book, *Treatise Concerning the Arte of Limning*, he records his conversations with the queen and his friendship with Sir Philip Sidney and Sir Christopher Hatton. His only existing correspondence is with Sir Robert Cecil, one of the queen's chief advisers. In 1591 Hilliard received £400, which may have been his fee for a portrait of the ill-fated Lady Arabella Stuart. If this is so, the picture has not been identified. Nor did the payment for it, large though it was, keep Hilliard out of debt.

On the death of Queen Elizabeth in 1603, Hilliard's patronage was taken over by her successor James I. The changed nature of the court, in which Elizabeth's elegance and assurance gave way to James's awkward earnestness, was reflected in Hilliard's work, which became more constrained and less obviously a pleasure to him. But he never lost his sureness of touch when painting a sympathetic sitter, particularly when his subject was as lovely a woman as Elizabeth of Bohemia.

In 1617 Hilliard was granted a 12-year monopoly of royal portraiture, and in the same year he was imprisoned in Ludgate for a debt. His troubles never soured him, however, and it is a gentle and likeable character that shows through the appalling complexity of style in his letters and his book. He was proud of his profession, considering limning to be a gentlemanly art. He says "it is sweet and cleanly to use, and it is a thing apart from all other painting or drawing, and tendeth not to common men's use." In 1619 he died, leaving his goods and his royal monopoly to his son Laurence, whom he affectionately believed to be as good a painter as himself.

N. Hilliard   *Treatise Concerning the Art of Limning*
    about 1600: published by the Walpole Society, Vol. I, Oxford, 1912
G. Reynolds   *Catalogue of the Nicholas Hilliard and Isaac Oliver Exhibition*
    *Victoria and Albert Museum, London, 1947*
J. Pope-Hennessy   *A Lecture on Nicholas Hilliard   London, 1949*
E. Auerbach   *Nicholas Hilliard   London, 1961*

Self-portrait, 1577
*London, V. and A.*

Queen Elizabeth, about 1600
*London, V. and A.*

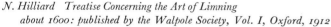

# WILLIAM HOGARTH                                    1697-1764

*A painter and engraver*

William Hogarth, the son of a schoolmaster who was an unsuccessful scholar, was born in the City of London, at Smithfield. His abundant autobiographical jottings show that even in childhood he had formed the habit of noting down his observations in rapid sketches. As a youth, he was apprenticed to an engraver of arms on silver. However, impressed by the work of James Thornhill in the Royal Hospital, Greenwich, and influenced by his notable success, Hogarth formed an ambition to succeed as a history painter.

In the 1720's, therefore, although he had started his own business as an engraver, he enrolled as a student in Vanderbank's Academy in St. Martin's Lane, and later he attended Thornhill's private art school in James Street, Covent Garden. There he met Thornhill's daughter, Jane, and in 1729, with his usual confidence and self-

Self-portrait, 1758
*London, N. P. G.*

Heads of Six of Hogarth's Servants
*London, N. G.*

Wm Hogarth

The Roast Beef of Old England:
Calais Gate (detail) 1748
*London, Tate*

assertion, he eloped with her. Throughout the 1720's Hogarth's income had come from book illustrations and satirical prints. When he married Jane Thornhill, the task of winning over her disapproving father may have strengthened his determination to improve his place in the hierarchy of artists. In 1730 he emerged as a painter of portraits and conversation pieces, one of which, the *Wanstead Assembly* executed between 1729 and 1731, contains no fewer than 25 portraits of the family and friends of Lord Castlemaine. By the beginning of 1731 he was well established in this field, orders poured in, and a list shows that at this time he had 16 commissions on hand. He was reconciled with his father-in-law.

Hogarth, however, regarded portraiture as a drudgery only a little better than engraving. He therefore turned his thoughts to "a more novel form of painting and engraving," that is, "the modern moral subject, a field not broken up in any country or in any age." These thoughts gave rise to his more famous works, those in which he proceeded as a dramatist, presenting a series of scenes to point a moral. The first of these, *The Harlot's Progress*, was engraved in 1732, and was followed by *The Rake's Progress* in 1735, and then, after a period of 10 years, by his masterpiece, *Marriage à la Mode*.

In 1734 Thornhill died and Hogarth inherited the art school. With his usual determination, he turned it into one of the most important English schools of art before the foundation of the Royal Academy in 1768. This was not the only effect of Thornhill's death on Hogarth; it re-awakened his ambition to be a history painter. No commissions were forthcoming, and so in 1735 he painted as a gift *The Pool of Bethesda* and *The Good Samaritan* for the staircase of St. Bartholomew's, the hospital of which he was a governor. No one was impressed, and, disappointed, Hogarth returned to the field of portraiture. The portrait of *Captain Coram*, his philanthropic friend, painted in 1740, is both the first and the finest example of middle class portraiture in the Grand Manner, displaying a combination of dignity derived from the Baroque tradition in Europe, and native directness. Hogarth supported Coram's projects for the Foundling Hospital, and in 1746 he organized for the hospital a permanent exhibition of paintings by British artists, which helped indirectly to popularize British art with the British public. During the 1740's Hogarth continued to be busy with portraits. Between 1743 and 1745 he was largely occupied with *Marriage à la Mode*, a series which more than any other shows his powers of satirical observation. In the first scene of this series, *The Contract*, every line speaks of the young man's fecklessness, his bride's indifference, and of the greed and condescension conflicting in his father. But his other satirical works were beginning to make him unpopular in some quarters, as was his constant warfare on second-rate European painting and on the charlatanism rife in picture dealing.

In 1749 Hogarth acquired a house at Chiswick and retired there to write his theoretical treatise, "The Analysis of Beauty," which was published in 1753. In England at least, it did nothing to brighten Hogarth's diminishing fame, which was now being eclipsed by Reynolds, just returned from Italy. Hogarth's roughly satirical *Election* series of 1754 fell far short of his earlier narrative series. In 1758 a picture ascribed to Correggio fetched a huge price in London. Hogarth rightly threw doubt on the attribution, but unwisely claimed that he could paint one just

The Beggar's Opera, about 1731
*London, Tate*

as good. The challenge was taken up by Sir Richard Grosvenor. Hogarth painted *Sigismunda*, which Sir Richard refused to buy, for though competent enough it was in his view well below European standards.

It is undoubtedly in unfinished works done for his own satisfaction, such as *The Shrimp Girl* and *Heads of Six of Hogarth's Servants*, that we see him at his finest. The acute observation that served him so well in satire gave a fresh sincerity to these portraits. But when he died in 1764 Hogarth was a disappointed man. He had been ambitious, and in his own eyes his ambitions had not been realized. He was in the unfortunate position of all pioneers, whose worth is of necessity unrealized during their lives.

*R. B. Beckett  Hogarth  London, 1949*
*F. Antal  Hogarth  London, 1962*

**HIS WORKS INCLUDE**

The Beggar's Opera, about 1731
*London, Tate*
Children Playing "The Indian Emperor" before an Audience, about 1732
*coll. Earl of Ilchester*
The Rake's Progress, 1735
*London, Soane Mus.*
Captain Coram, 1740
*London, Coram Foundation*
Marriage à la Mode, about 1745
*London, N. G.*
The Shrimp Girl
*London, N. G.*
Heads of Six of Hogarth's Servants
*London, N. G.*

**See also pages 96, 97, 98, 168**

---

# JAMES HOLLAND                                    1800-1870

*A landscape and flower painter*

Holland was born at Burslem in Staffordshire. As a young man he painted flowers on porcelain, and at the age of 19 went to London, where he lived by teaching and making small flower paintings. These he exhibited at the Royal Academy from 1824. It was as the result of a journey to Paris that Holland took up landscape painting. He then visited various parts of the continent, finding on his journeys his ideal subject matter. Much of his best work was done in Venice. He took part in the exhibitions of the Society of Painters in Watercolor, in those of the British Artists, and in those held by the British Institution. He died in London in 1870.

**HIS WORKS INCLUDE**

The Rialto, Venice
*Edinburgh, N. G. of Scotland*
Hyde Park Corner, looking East, about 1840
*London, Tate*

**See also page 185**

## ARTHUR HUGHES

1832-1915

*A painter associated with the Pre-Raphaelite movement*

Arthur Hughes entered the Royal Academy Schools in 1847. In 1849 he showed his first exhibited work, *Musidora*, an undistinguished figure painting in the contemporary academic style. In 1850 he met William Holman Hunt, Dante Gabriel Rossetti, and Ford Madox Brown, and he became converted to the theory of the Pre-Raphaelite Brotherhood. In 1852 he met John Everett Millais, the year in which he showed his own Pre-Raphaelite picture, *Ophelia*.

Hughes' best work belongs to the 1850's and early 1860's. A man of retiring and gentle nature, his painting was delicate and poetic. In 1857 he worked with William Morris on the decoration of the Union at Oxford University. In the following year he left London and the society of other artists for a quiet home in the suburbs, where he retired into obscurity. His later works became feebly sentimental and uninteresting. Hughes' life was happy and, save for a visit to Italy in 1862, uneventful.

*R. Ironside and J. Gere   Pre-Raphaelite Painters   London, 1948*

Home from the Sea, 1863
*Oxford, Ashmolean Mus.*

HIS WORKS INCLUDE

April Love, 1856
*London, Tate*

The Long Engagement, 1859
*Birmingham, England, City Art Gall.*

**See also page 146**

## WILLIAM HOLMAN HUNT

1827-1910

*The most faithful member of the Pre-Raphaelite Brotherhood*

As a young man William Holman Hunt spent his leisure hours studying the exhibitions at the British Museum and the National Gallery, and sketching out of doors. At the age of 16 he began to devote all his time to painting, and he entered the Royal Academy Schools in 1844.

Hunt met John Everett Millais at the Royal Academy and with him helped to found the Pre-Raphaelite Brotherhood in 1848. The same year he exhibited *The Flight of Madeleine and Porphyro*, a scene from Keats's poem, "The Eve of St. Agnes." Hunt interpreted the scene as "the sacredness of honest responsible love, and the weakness of proud intemperance," and he sought to represent it in appropriate, if ungainly, actions. Unlike Millais, Hunt remained faithful to the ideals of the Pre-Raphaelites: to have genuine ideas to express; to study directly from nature, disregarding all arbitrary rules; and to envisage events as they must have happened, rather than as the rules of design required.

*The Light of the World*, Hunt's most famous religious work, was exhibited at the Academy in 1864. Hunt visited Palestine several times. *The Awakening Conscience*, also exhibited in 1864, demonstrates his belief in the moral content of pictures. His late works were very detailed, often weighed down by over-elaboration. Some of them were repainted towards the end of his long life and this makes them difficult to judge. Hunt's memoirs expounded his theory of painting.

*W. Holman Hunt   The Pre-Raphaelite Brotherhood   London, 1905*
*R. Ironside and J. Gere   Pre-Raphaelite Painters   London, 1948*

Self-portrait, 1845
*Birmingham, England, City Art Gall.*

HIS WORKS INCLUDE

The Awakening Conscience, 1854
*London, coll. Sir Colin Anderson*

The Light of the World, 1854
*Oxford, Keble College*

The Scapegoat, 1856
*Port Sunlight, England,
Lady Lever Art Gall.*

The Hireling Shepherd, 1851
*Manchester, England, City Art Gall.*

**See also page 141**

## GEORGE INNESS

1825-1894

*An American landscape painter*

George Inness was largely self-taught. He was an epileptic and a visionary, and his painting sprang mainly from his own temperament and disposition. His trips to Europe, in 1847 and 1851, 1859 and 1871-75, opened his eyes to a variety of artistic styles and types of landscape. In 1859 he settled in a small village in eastern Massachusetts, where the countryside reminded him of Barbizon in France. He was much influenced by Corot and produced works similar in style to the Barbizon School. His paintings at this stage were extremely naturalistic in conception, and atmosphere and light greatly preoccupied him.

In the 1860's and 1870's Inness' palette changed and became more sultry. Feeling that he needed new subject matter, he went to Italy, and his paintings of the Roman countryside brought him new success and popularity. When he returned to America he continued to paint in a suffused style which had certain similarities to Impressionism. His late work was a reversal of his former style, and until his death in 1894 Inness' paintings were an important element in the revulsion against the naturalism of the late 19th century.

*F. McCausland   George Inness, and American Landscape Painters, 1825-1894   New York, 1946*

HIS WORKS INCLUDE

Delaware Water Gap, 1861
*New York, Met. Mus.*
Harvest Time, 1864
*Cleveland, Mus. of Art*
The Coming Storm, 1878
*Buffalo, Art Gall.*
The Home of the Heron, 1893
*Chicago, Art. Inst.*

**See also page 160**

The Lackawanna Valley, 1855
*Washington, D.C., Nat. Gall. of Art*

---

## INIGO JONES

1573-1651

*An architect and designer for the stage*

Inigo Jones was born in London on July 15, 1573. He made early studies in landscape painting, but soon turned to architecture. The work of the 16th-century architects, Palladio and Scamozzi, particularly interested him.

In 1604 Jones went to Denmark. He returned to England the next year, bringing with him a recommendation from Christian IV of Denmark to his brother-in-law James I of England. Almost immediately Jones was employed by Oxford University to stage three plays for the king, and he was commissioned to collaborate with Ben Jonson on the "Masque of Blackness."

After his second Italian trip in 1614, Jones was made surveyor-general to the king. He prepared designs for the new palace at Whitehall that were never put into practice in their entirety. The Banqueting House was finished in 1622 and expressed all Jones had learned in Italy. The later publication of his designs contributed to the distinctive Palladian trend of British 18th-century architecture. The Tuscan portico of St. Paul's Church, Covent Garden, and the Queen's House. Greenwich, were also designed by Jones, and various great houses show his hand, After the Civil War he had to pay the penalty for his royal employment; he was fined heavily and died in poverty on July 5, 1651.

*J. Lees-Milne   The Age of Inigo Jones   London, 1953*
*J. A. Gotch   Inigo Jones   London, 1928*

The Queen's House, 1616-35
*London, Greenwich*

**See also pages 163, 164**

## SIR GODFREY KNELLER

Self-portrait
*London, N. P. G.*

*A portrait painter who dominated English art for forty years*

Godfrey Kneller was born in Lübeck, probably in 1649. His talent was recognized early, and in 1666 he was sent to study in Amsterdam, where he may have met Rembrandt. From Holland he traveled to Rome, where he met some of the leading Italian painters of the day, notably Giovanni Baciccia and Carlo Maratta.

In 1674 Kneller went to London with a recommendation to Jonathan Banks, a Hamburg merchant. Seeing some of his work displayed in Banks' house, James Vernon, secretary to the Duke of Monmouth, decided to have his portrait painted. After Vernon it was a natural step for Kneller to paint the duke, and eventually the king himself. In the early 1680's Kneller's mature style emerged. The best of these early portraits, notably that of James II done in 1684, show a simplicity of background and tone, restraint in posture, and a sobriety of color, which may well have made a welcome contrast to the flamboyance of Sir Peter Lely. Kneller was fully able to succeed Lely as the dominant painter in London and to take over his fashionable practice. He organized his team of assistants to the best advantage, his health was excellent, and he was a quick worker. His arrogance and violent temper, however, were proverbial.

By 1685 Kneller was well enough established to be referred to by the diarist John Evelyn as "the famous painter." He had been to France to make a portrait of Louis XIV, and in 1688 he was appointed, with John Riley, first painter to William and Mary. In 1694 Kneller began a series of full length portraits known as the *Hampton Court Beauties*, and in the early 1700's a series of admirals at Greenwich, which do not compare in quality with Lely's. Kneller's best and most justly

John Dryden (detail)
*Cambridge, Trinity College*

James II, 1684
*London, N. P. G.*

The First Marquess of Tweeddale, 1695
*London, Tate*

48

famous set of paintings is the *Kit-Cat* series, painted between 1702 and 1717. These 42 portraits are of the members of the Kit-Cat Club, a social group comprised of members of the Whig party. All the portraits are 36 by 28 inches, a size that allows for head and shoulders and one hand, and the name Kit-Cat has since always been given to this type of portrait.

In 1711 Kneller became the first governor of the first academy of painting in London. This school established a sound studio tradition for the next generation; in particular, the practice of having numerous assistants who specialized in wigs, draperies, lace, landscape, architecture and a host of other features. In his own right, however, Kneller dominated the English portrait painting of his era.

*E. K. Waterhouse  Painting in Britain, 1530-1790  London, 1953*

HIS WORKS INCLUDE

James, Duke of Monmouth, 1678
*Goodwood, England,*
*coll. Duke of Richmond and Gordon*
Hampton Court Beauties, from 1694
*Hampton Court, Royal Coll.*
Admirals, 1700-10
*Greenwich, London, Nat. Maritime Mus.*
John Dryden
*Cambridge, Trinity College*
Kit-Cat Series, 1702-17
*London, N. P. G.*

**See also pages 94, 166**

# CORNELIUS KRIEGHOFF                    1815-1872

*A painter of Canadian frontier scenes*

Cornelius Krieghoff was probably born in Düsseldorf. He apparently studied in German art schools and in Rotterdam. In 1833 he settled in Quebec, although he spent some years traveling around Europe, visiting London at least once, and in 1837 New York.

Krieghoff became one of the first painters to depict the Canadian landscape. He painted numerous canvases of life in the province of Quebec, and many of his works depict drinking parties in roadside taverns which are lively in subject but rather stereotyped in technique. Adriaen van Ostade's Dutch peasant scenes are an obvious influence. Krieghoff's best work was produced between 1856 and 1860, notably autumn landscapes and sunsets. He painted Indians in forest settings and occasionally depicted early trains and steamships.

In his later years Krieghoff made copies of his paintings rather than fresh compositions in order to meet the demand for his work, which was particularly popular with the English garrison officers. He had many lithographs and engravings made from his paintings when such prints were fashionable. After 1834 he exhibited with the short-lived Toronto Society of Artists. He died in 1872.

*ed. R. H. Hubbard  An Anthology of Canadian Art  Toronto, 1960*

Settler's Log Cabin (detail) 1856
*Toronto, Art Gall.*

HIS WORKS INCLUDE

Winter Landscape, 1849
*Ottawa, N. G. of Canada*
Settler's Log Cabin, 1856
*Toronto, Art. Gall.*
Merrymaking, 1860
*Fredericton, New Brunswick,*
*Beaverbrook Art Gall.*

**See also page 159**

# SIR EDWIN LANDSEER                    1802-1873

*An animal painter*

Edwin Landseer was the son of an engraver who taught his three sons to draw. Edwin studied animal anatomy by dissecting and showed an early talent for animal painting. He exhibited *Fighting Dogs Getting Wind* at the Society of Painters in

**See also page 137**

SIR F. GRANT
Portrait of Sir Edwin Landseer
(detail) 1852
*London, N. P. G.*

Oil and Watercolor when he was 16 and was thereafter referred to by his master Henry Fuseli as "my curly-headed dog boy." In 1821 *Rat Catchers* was shown at the Royal Academy; it is a lively, vigorous work showing the vitality of Landseer's early painting. In 1824, however, he painted and exhibited *The Cat's Paw*, a work which was to become fatally popular. Its subject is singularly horrible—a monkey has seized a cat, which shrieks in terror, in order to use its paw to move hot chestnuts off a stove. This wildly successful painting set the pattern for the pathetic, sentimental, and grotesque animals for which Landseer is famed.

For the rest of his life Landseer's popularity neither waned, nor was questioned. During the 1830's he painted a series of Highland subjects, one of which, *The Old Shepherd's Chief Mourner*, was called by John Ruskin "one of the most perfect poems or pictures (I use the words as synonymous) which modern times have seen." Landseer was also a favorite of Queen Victoria. He painted with ever greater facility, and ever less real feeling. In 1850 he was knighted and all possible honors were to be heaped upon him. He was awarded a gold medal at the Paris Universal Exhibition of 1855, and was offered, but refused, the presidency of the Royal Academy in 1865. One of the most notable achievements of his last years was the modeling of the lions that surround Nelson's Column in Trafalgar Square, London.

*J. Woodward Catalogue of the Landseer Exhibition Royal Academy, London, 1961*

---

## MARCELLUS LAROON THE YOUNGER          1679-1774

*A witty draftsman of the 18th-century scene*

Marcellus Laroon was born in London, and was trained in the tradition of his father, a Dutch artist who had settled in England. Despite this background, he never became a professional artist, though he was an able and prolific draftsman. In 1707 he joined the army and saw service under Marlborough in Flanders, and later fought in Spain and against the Old Pretender in 1715. His lively drawings of soldiers give substance to the contemporary complaint that Marlborough's soldiers "swore horribly."

On leaving the army Laroon settled in London and lived as an occasional actor and man-about-town. He drew scenes of everyday urban life, which vibrate with acute observation and a kind of staccato wit. His few paintings are very deficient in color, being almost monochromatic, and look like drawings in oil. After a long and active life, he died in Oxford.

Many of Laroon's drawings are in the British Museum, London, and in the Ashmolean Museum, Oxford.

**See also page 167**

---

## SIR THOMAS LAWRENCE          1769-1830

*The most celebrated English portrait painter of his day*

Thomas Lawrence was born in Bristol in 1769. He was exceptionally precocious, and by the age of 12 he was already in practice at Bath drawing portraits in crayon.

In 1787 Lawrence became a student in the Royal Academy Schools and began to show in its annual exhibitions. He was devoted to the teaching of Sir Joshua Reynolds and he longed to paint histories in the Grand Manner, but could not attain to it. He turned to portraiture reluctantly, but his facility for an elegant likeness ensured his popularity. On Reynolds' death in 1792, Lawrence was appointed painter-in-ordinary to the king in his place, and he had no serious competition after the death of John Hoppner in 1810. Some of Lawrence's works, such as *The Princess of Wales and the Princess Charlotte*, suffer from his hankering for the Grand Style. This work in particular is theatrically posed. On the other hand his stage portraits, especially of John Kemble, are more natural in their romanticism.

Lawrence was knighted by the prince regent in 1815, and between 1814 and 1819 was commissioned by him to paint all the chief personalities of the wars against Napoleon. The portraits were begun in London in 1814 and their glitter and force established Lawrence's European reputation. Possibly his finest work, in that it is the most subtle psychological study, is his portrait of Pope Pius VII, which hangs, with the others in the series, in the Waterloo Chamber at Windsor Castle. Lawrence returned to London from Rome in 1820 to be elected president of the Royal Academy. Some of his best works belong to his later years, when he had achieved a synthesis of style. On his death in 1830 his superb collection of Old Master drawings was offered to the English nation on very easy terms, but through the gross ineptitude of the government department concerned it was refused and the collection was dispersed.

D. E. Williams   *Life and Correspondence of Sir Thomas Lawrence*   *London, 1831*
D. Goldring   *Regency Portrait Painters*   *London, 1951*
K. J. Garlick   *Lawrence*   *London, 1954*

Self-portrait (detail)
*London, R. A.*

## HIS WORKS INCLUDE

Queen Charlotte, 1790
*London, N. G.*

Miss Farren, 1790
*New York, Met. Mus.*

Sir Francis Baring
and his Partners, 1807
*coll. Lord Northbrook*

The Waterloo Chamber Portraits,
1814-30
*Windsor, Royal Coll.*

Lady Peel, 1827
*New York, Frick Coll.*

**See also pages 124, 125, 182**

Thomas Campbell
*London, N. P. G.*

Samuel Rogers
*London, N. P. G.*

Queen Charlotte (detail) 1790
*London, N. G.*

W. N. MARSTRAND
Portrait of Edward Lear (detail) 1840
*London, N. P. G.*

HIS WORKS INCLUDE
Valmontone, 1839
*London, B. M.*
Tivoli from the West, 1840
*London, B. M.*

**See also page 187**

# EDWARD LEAR
1812-1888

*A landscape artist more famous for his verse for children*

Edward Lear was born in London in 1812. From the age of 15 he earned money by drawing local scenes and birds and flowers. In 1832 he published *Illustrations of the Family of Psittacidae*, with 42 plates made from drawings executed in the bird house of the London Zoo. The Earl of Derby employed Lear to draw the menagerie at Knowsley, and it was for the earl's children that Lear composed his first *Book of Nonsense*.

In 1837 Lear went to Italy. He spent ten years in Rome and visited many parts of the Mediterranean. During this period he published his *Illustrated Journals of a Landscape Painter*. Queen Victoria took drawing lessons from him when he returned to England in 1845, but by 1848 he was exploring the Near East, and in 1854 and 1855 he visited Egypt, Corfu, and Malta. He spent 1873 to 1875 in India and Ceylon, where he made many drawings.

Lear's work is delicate and accurate and the illustrations to his *Nonsense* books are as vivacious as his writing and conversation. He died in his villa at San Remo in 1888.

*A. Davidson   Edward Lear   London, 1938*

Self-portrait (detail) 1650-55
*London, N. P. G.*

*Lely*

# SIR PETER LELY
1618-1680

*A fashionable portrait painter*

Peter Lely was born in Soest in Westphalia of Dutch parents. He studied in Haarlem, Holland, and in 1637 he became master of the Haarlem guild. He arrived in London either in 1641, in time for the marriage of William of Orange and the Princess Mary Stuart, or in 1643.

In 1647 Lely received his first royal commission for a portrait. Charles I's children were allowed to visit him in his imprisonment at Hampton Court, and Lely painted the king with James, Duke of York. He also painted a group portrait of the three youngest children, who were in the care of the Earl of Northumberland.

During the ten years of the Commonwealth, Lely continued to prosper. He painted many mythological subjects, and in 1651 demonstrated his political adap-

The Children of Charles I, about 1647
*Petworth, England*

tability with a proposal to decorate Whitehall with pictures of Parliament's achievements. This project collapsed, but from 1653 Lely painted portraits of Cromwell and carried on his earlier practice of painting history and subject pieces and even religious pictures. He moderated his style to suit the austere taste of the Commonwealth.

Lely made a trip to Holland in 1656, and possibly made some contact with the exiled court, for upon the restoration of the English monarchy in 1660 he was at once appointed as first painter to the king. He evolved a new style to agree with the new taste, and by 1671 he was charging £20 for a head, £30 for a half length portrait, and £60 for a full length. He coped with a flood of work; sittings began at 7 o'clock in the morning, assistants painted accessories, drapery, and background detail. The gesturing Baroque postures in which his subjects posed were designated by numbers, so that an entry in Lely's order book might read "58 Lord Arran (ye Ladie 57)."

In spite of these production line methods, Lely never let his technique slip. During the 1660's he painted two sets of portraits, a series of admirals at Greenwich, and a series of court ladies, done at the queen's request, known as the *Windsor Beauties*. Samuel Pepys confided to his diary that the painter was "a mighty proud man ..... and full of state." Lely's pride was justified in that his success was unrivalled among his contemporaries and he exactly caught the sensual languor to which the court aspired. "None but my Lilly ever drew a Minde" wrote the poet Richard Lovelace. In 1679 Lely was knighted. In the following year he died and was buried at St. Paul's Church, Covent Garden.

*R. B. Beckett Lely London, 1951*
*E. K. Waterhouse Painting in Britain, 1530-1790 London, 1953*

One of the Windsor Beauties, about 1668
*Hampton Court, Royal Coll.*

HIS WORKS INCLUDE
Charles I and the Duke of York, 1647
*Middlesex, England,*
*Syon House, coll. Duke of Northumberland*
The Children of Charles I, about 1647
*Petworth, England*
Admiral Sir Jeremy Smith, 1666-67
*Greenwich, London, Nat. Maritime Mus.*
Windsor Beauties, about 1668
*Hampton Court, Royal Coll.*

**See also pages 93, 165**

---

## HUBERT LE SUEUR       active 1610-1643, died 1670

*A French sculptor who worked at the English Court*

Little is known of Hubert Le Sueur's origins or training. He was reputed to have been the pupil of Giovanni da Bologna, the Mannerist sculptor from Flanders who worked in Italy, but this is unlikely. He was, however, well enough established by 1619 to hold the title *sculpteur du roi* in France. He went to England from France at the end of the 1620's, and lived in the Huguenot colony in London. He stayed in London until the Civil War, making only occasional trips to Paris to search for statuary for Charles I.

Le Sueur's works include an equestrian statue of Charles I, made for a garden at Roehampton, but finally set up at Charing Cross in 1678, a figure of Mercury, for a fountain, a bust of Charles I, and a bust of James I. In 1643, on a trip to France, Le Sueur made for the Duchess of Aiguillon, the niece of Cardinal Richelieu, four bronze busts of the cardinal, after models by Jean Warin. He returned to England after the Civil War, and died in London in 1670.

*M. Whinney and O. Millar English Art, 1625-1714 Oxford, 1957*

Charles I
*London, V. and A.*

HIS WORKS INCLUDE
Charles I
*London, V. and A.*
Equestrian Statue of Charles I, 1633
*London, Charing Cross*

**See also page 197**

## JOHN BAPTIST MALCHAIR

1731-1812

*A topographer of Oxford*

John Malchair was born in Cologne, coming to England in about 1754. He began teaching drawing and music in Lewes, and in 1758 and 1759 lived in Bristol, where he made many sketches. He eventually settled permanently in Oxford. He became a prominent musician there and also built up a practice as a drawing master, teaching some distinguished amateurs. He gave his practice to William Delamotte on the failure of his eyesight in 1799.

Malchair made his reputation as a topographer of Oxford. His earlier work shows an appreciation of striking visual and atmospheric effects, and his visits to Wales gave his work greater breadth and an appreciation of massive forms. He worked frequently in pencil, or gray and brown wash, and in his later years explored the possibilities of imaginative landscape. He died on December 12, 1812.

*I. A. Williams Early English Watercolors London, 1952*

A Bridge and Trees *London, B. M.*

**HIS WORKS INCLUDE**

St. Barnabas, Oxford, 1782
*Oxford, Ashmolean*
Oxford in Flood Time,
from Shotover Hill, 1791
*Oxford, Ashmolean*

**See also page 171**

---

## BENJAMIN MARSHALL

1767-1835

*A horse painter and writer of sporting articles*

Ben Marshall was born in Leicestershire and was trained as a portrait painter. In 1792 he began to paint the works for which he is best remembered, hunting and racing pictures. He went to London, where he drew horse-portraits for *The Sporting Magazine*, and soon built up a large circle of patrons, among them the Prince of Wales, whose hunters he painted.

From 1801 Marshall occasionally exhibited his paintings of horses at the Royal Academy and sometimes showed a portrait. He worked in London until 1812 and then moved to Newmarket, where his beautifully modeled works continued to be successful. In 1819 Marshall suffered a bad accident when the coach in which he was traveling overturned. He never entirely recovered his health, and his painting deteriorated. From 1821, therefore, until the end of his life, he gave up painting almost entirely but contributed articles to *Sporting Magazine* under the *nom de plume* "Observator."

*W. S. Sparrow British Sporting Artists London, 1922*

**HIS WORKS INCLUDE**

F. D. Astley and his Harriers, 1809
*Upton House, Oxfordshire, National Trust*
Anticipation and Bourbon, 1817
*Cottesbrooke Hall,
coll. Major R. Macdonald-Buchanan*

**See also page 121**

---

## SIR JOHN EVERETT MILLAIS

1829-1896

*A founder-member of the Pre-Raphaelite Brotherhood*

John Everett Millais was the son of a Jersey family of French extraction, and showed all the signs of being an infant prodigy. He entered the Royal Academy Schools in 1840, and there he met William Holman Hunt. The two artists became good friends, recognizing in one another a fellow spirit; artistically both were revolutionaries.

In 1848 Hunt painted a scene from Keats's poem "The Eve of St. Agnes," *The Flight of Madeleine and Porphyro.* Dante Gabriel Rossetti shared Millais' and Hunt's admiration for Keats, and he liked Hunt's picture. The three artists joined together to found the Pre-Raphaelite Brotherhood. In 1850 Millais painted *Christ in the House of His Parents,* a work which shows the Pre-Raphaelite ideal of realism in religious paintings. Millais' technical accomplishment had been demonstrated by his painting of *Isabella and Lorenzo,* a rhythmic composition of considerable intensity. Technically he outdistanced the other members of the Pre-Raphaelite Brotherhood, and he gradually forsook Pre-Raphaelite theories. In 1853 he was elected an associate of the Royal Academy. He became a fashionable and brilliant academic painter of portraits, popular themes, and genre subjects. By the 1860's, however, his work had degenerated, becoming over-sentimental and extremely facile. His technical ability remained, giving all his work a certain distinction, and there are many very good portraits dating from his later years. In 1864 Millais became a full member of the Royal Academy, and in 1896 was its president for a few months before his death.

*J. G. Millais  Life and Letters of Sir John Everett Millais  London, 1900*
*R. Ironside and J. Gere  Pre-Raphaelite Painters  London, 1948*

CHARLES KEENE
Portrait of Sir John Millais
*London, N. P. G.*

Ophelia, 1852
*London, Tate*

**HIS WORKS INCLUDE**

Christ in the House of his Parents, 1850
*London, Tate*
The Blind Girl, 1856
*Birmingham, England, City Art Gall.*
Autumn Leaves, 1856
*Manchester, England, City Art Gall.*
Ophelia, 1852
*London, Tate*
The North-West Passage, 1874
*London, Tate*

**See also pages 145, 188**

## GEORGE MORLAND                                    1763-1804

*A painter of rural life*

George Morland was the son of a painter and engraver of good reputation and sound income. Showing an early talent for drawing, he was kept hard at work by his father from the age of 14. His early productions were chiefly illustrations, for example for Spenser's "Faerie Queene," which were sold to engravers.

**HIS WORKS INCLUDE**

Inside of a Stable, about 1790
*London, Tate*
The Ale House Door, 1792
*Edinburgh, N. G. of Scotland*
Pigs, 1797
*Birmingham, England, City Art Gall.*

**See also page 120**

Rabbiting (detail) 1792
*London, Tate*

Long Island Farmhouse (detail)
after 1854
*New York, Met. Mus. of Art*

HIS WORKS INCLUDE

Bargaining for a Horse, 1835
*New York, Hist. Soc.*

The Painter's Triumph, 1836
*Philadelphia, Acad. of Fine Arts*

**See also pages 156, 192**

At the age of 19 Morland, who was high-spirited and melancholy by turns, began to evade his father's discipline. He fell into debt, and was forced to turn to hack work. He became popular for his picturesque paintings of rustic scenes, but his popularity was exploited by agents to whom he owed money. In 1786 he married the sister of an engraver named Ward, who had been good to him, and a period of steady industry ensued. His best works were done between 1788 and 1798—pictures of peasants, animals, and stable interiors. The good effect of his marriage was short-lived. He was blessed with natural talent and effortless ability, but, painting between bouts of dissipation, he never developed his gifts. Even so, he turned his low associates to good account, using them as models.

In 1799 Morland was arrested while on the run from his creditors, and his health broke down. Though released in 1802, he despaired and proceeded to drink himself to death. He died at the age of 41, declaring that his epitaph should be "Here lies a drunken dog." Although not in the first rank of English artists, Morland had shown that the English peasantry could be as picturesque as the Italian and that there was a public for paintings of this genre.

*G. C. Williamson  George Morland  London, 1907*

## WILLIAM SIDNEY MOUNT                    1807-1868

*A painter of simple and natural country scenes*

William Sidney Mount grew up in the country town of Stony Brook on Long Island in New York. He was born in 1807 in neighboring Setauket, and in 1826 he went to the drawing classes recently begun by the National Academy of Design. He studied there until he was forced to go home because of illness. On his return he realized the many pictorial possibilities of his home country, and he returned to this for his subject matter, instead of continuing to paint portraits and religious scenes. From this time on he needed no further stimulus than the landscape and the life around him. Mount, unlike many of his contemporaries, had no wish to travel to Europe. He worked hard to achieve the greatest possible technical ability, and was outstanding in his feeling for line and in his drawing, which was lively and full of movement. His paintings were always simply composed and the coloring clear and glowing. Mount's attitude to his subject offers a parallel to that of Washington Irving in literature.

*B. Cowdray and H. W. Williams, Jr.  William Sidney Mount  New York, 1944*

## DANIEL MYTENS                    about 1590 - before 1648

*A Dutch-born painter who worked at the English court*

Daniel Mytens was born in about 1590 and trained at The Hague. He matriculated in the guild in 1610 and by 1618 he was in London. He at first worked under the patronage of Thomas Howard, Earl of Arundel, a connoisseur who wished to "marry" European and English art, and in 1619 he began to receive royal commissions. In 1623 there is a recorded payment for portraits of King James I, and his son, Charles. When Charles came to the throne he made Mytens painter to the crown and Mytens was then fully employed producing royal portraits, many of them for dispatch to foreign courts.

In 1626 Mytens returned to the Low Countries. This short visit enabled him to acquaint himself with the latest fashions in Flemish portraiture, profoundly affecting his style. The portraits of the late 1620's and early 1630's, for example *The Duke of Buckingham*, 1626, and *The First Duke of Hamilton*, 1629, show that a study of the elegances of Sir Anthony van Dyck had eliminated the stiffness apparent in his earlier work.

In 1632 van Dyck returned to England and pleased the king by an elegant portrayal. Mytens' last known royal portrait was painted in 1633. He returned to Holland two years later and no works by him exist after this date.

*E. K. Waterhouse   Painting in Britain, 1530-1790   London, 1953*

**HIS WORKS INCLUDE**

Martha, Countess of Monmouth
*Knole, England, coll. Lord Sackville*

The Earl of Arundel, 1618
*Arundel Castle, Sussex, England, coll. Duke of Norfolk*

Prince Charles, about 1623
*Windsor, Royal Coll.*

2nd Earl of Warwick, 1632
*Greenwich, London, Nat. Maritime Mus.*

**See also page 89**

## JOSEPH NOLLEKENS                1737-1823

*A sculptor of portrait busts*

Joseph Nollekens was the second son of Joseph Francis Nollekens, a painter. In 1750 he was apprenticed to the sculptor Scheemakers, whose industrious pupil he became. In 1759 he won a prize from the Society of Arts for a drawing from plaster. A year later he won first prize for a clay model of *Jeptha's Rash Vow*.

In 1760 Nollekens traveled to Rome, where he settled for some time. In 1762 he sent a marble relief of *Timocles Conducted before Alexander* to England, which gained him a prize from the Society of Arts. During his stay in Rome he also began to deal in terracottas and antique fragments, which he restored and sold to collectors from England. In 1770 he decided to go back to England, making a short visit to Paris on the way.

In London Nollekens set up a studio in Mortimer Street, and received numerous commissions from London's fashionable society. He made a great reputation as a sculptor, comparable with that of Reynolds as a painter. Among his commissions were many sculptured decorations for country houses. He worked also in plaster, and in 1775 was paid £280 for decorating the Great Hall of Drapers' Hall.

Among Nollekens' portrait busts the most famous were those of the statesmen William Pitt and Charles Fox. He exhibited at the Royal Academy from 1771 to 1816. In 1771 he was elected an associate, and in the following year he was made a member. He died on April 23, 1823.

*J. T. Smith   Nollekens and his Times   London, 1828*
*R. Gunnis   Dictionary of British Sculptors   London, 1953*

L. F. ABBOTT
Portrait of Joseph Nollekens
*London, N. P. G.*

**HIS WORKS INCLUDE**

Medusa, 1764
*London, R. A.*

Castor and Pollux, 1768
*London, V. and A.*

Monument to Oliver Goldsmith, 1774
*London, Westminster Abbey*

Monument to Colonel Charles Macleod, 1812
*London, Westminster Abbey*

**See also page 204**

## JOHN VAN NOST                                        died 1729

HIS WORKS INCLUDE

Two Statues of Amorini, about 1706
*Melbourne Hall, Derbyshire, England*

George I, 1717
*Birmingham, England, Barber Inst.*

Monument to 3rd Earl of Bristol, 1698
*Sherborne, England, Abbey*

**See also page 200**

*An ornamental sculptor*

John van Nost came to England from Malines and took over the business of the Flemish sculptor Arnold Quellin. He made many different articles in lead, and for Thomas Coke, one of his first patrons, he made figures, fountain decorations, and the large *Vase of the Seasons*. The statues on the pediment of Buckingham House, mentioned in 18th-century guide books to London, were also his work.

Records of van Nost's work for Hampton Court mention models for fountains, statuary, marble tables and chimney pieces. He executed five equestrian statues of George I, one being erected on the Grattan Bridge, Dublin. His most outstanding monument is of 1711, commemorating the Duke of Queensberry. The columns of the baldachino are based on those in the Raphael cartoons in the Royal Collection; on the tomb Queensberry lies on his side, gazing down at the Duchess, who had died two years earlier. Van Nost died in 1729.

*R. Gunnis   Dictionary of British Sculptors   London, 1953*

---

## ISAAC OLIVER                                         died 1617

Self-portrait
*Cambridge, Fitzwm.*

HIS WORKS INCLUDE

A Young Man (Sir Philip Sidney?), about 1590
*Windsor, Royal Coll.*

Robert Devereux, Earl of Essex, about 1595
*Windsor, Royal Coll.*

Henry Frederick, Prince of Wales
*Windsor, Royal Coll.*

Richard Sackville, 3rd Earl of Dorset, 1616
*London, V. and A.*

**See also pages 88, 162**

*A miniaturist contemporary with Hilliard*

As a baby Isaac Oliver was brought from Rouen by his father, a Huguenot goldsmith, to escape from religious persecution. The family came to England in 1568, and by 1595 Oliver had become the rival of his master, Nicholas Hilliard. Although he was Hilliard's pupil, Oliver's style could hardly have been more different. While Hilliard's miniatures are painted in clear colors, against light backgrounds and with the lightest of modeling, Oliver's are dark in tone and more heavily shaded. With the accession of James I in 1603, Oliver's style became increasingly popular, and he received as many royal commissions as Hilliard, the official limner to the king.

It is possible that Oliver traveled abroad in 1588, and an inscription on the back of a portrait entitled *Sir Arundell Talbot* records a visit to Venice in 1596. He was married three times in all; in 1594 his first wife bore him his eldest son, Peter, who was to become almost as good a miniaturist as his father. In 1602 he married Sara, the daughter of the Flemish painter Marc Gheeraerts, who had brought his family to England at about the same time as the Olivers. His third wife was called Elizabeth, and she lived long enough to become his executrix. It is probable that she, too, was of a family of painters.

Little else is known of Oliver's life, and little of his character, except what may be gleaned from his self-portraits, which show him in the dress and attitude of a dandy. He died in 1617, leaving all his drawings "finished and unfinished" to his son Peter. In one case at least, Peter completed his father's work, and it is most probable that father and son had often worked together.

*G. Reynolds   Catalogue of the Nicholas Hilliard and Isaac Oliver Exhibition*
   *Victoria and Albert Museum London, 1947*

# SAMUEL PALMER
1805-1881

*A follower of William Blake*

Samuel Palmer's father was a poor bookseller who educated his son personally, except for two very unhappy terms at the Merchant Taylors' School in London. The artist's education was based on the Bible and Milton, with a little Latin. His first drawing master was William Wate, an obscure topographical painter.

In 1819 Palmer exhibited at the British Institution and the Royal Academy conventional romantic views influenced by the works of Cox and Turner. In 1824 he became a disciple of William Blake, whom he met at the home of John Linnell. He fell under the power of Blake's world, in Palmer's words, of "visions of little dells and nooks and corners of paradise." After Blake's death a group of his young followers continued to meet at Shoreham in Kent, where Palmer lived with his father between 1826 and 1835. During this time he reached the peak of his creative power. His pastoral landscapes of these years are transfigured by the mysticism he had learned from Blake, and they became symbols of perfect rural peace.

In 1837 Palmer married Linnell's daughter and visited Italy. This marked the end of his visionary works. He never again achieved a unique vision; although the golden Claude-like landscapes of his last years were never without distinction, he had lost what he had termed his "primitive and infantile" feeling for landscapes.

A. H. Palmer  *Life and Letters of Samuel Palmer*  London, 1892
G. Grigson  *Samuel Palmer, the Visionary Years*  London, 1947

GEORGE RICHMOND
Portrait of Samuel Palmer
*London, N. P. G.*

SAMUEL PALMER

HIS WORKS INCLUDE

In a Shoreham Garden, about 1829
*London, V. and A.*
Coming from Evening Church, 1830
*London, Tate*
The Harvest Moon, about 1833
*London, Tate*

**See also pages 138, 180, 181**

---

# CHARLES WILLSON PEALE
1741-1827

*An artist of varied interests, important for his innovations in museum organization*

Charles Willson Peale was born in Queen Anne's County, Maryland. He was apprenticed to a saddler and experimented with many crafts, including silversmithing and brass casting. In Norfolk, Virginia, he saw works which determined him to paint. Friends raised enough money for him to study in London with Benjamin West in 1766 and 1767.

Peale then settled in Philadelphia and he became an eminent portrait painter. His sitters included George Washington, and Peale decided to produce a complete range of portraits of outstanding men of his time. After 1781 he built an exhibition gallery near his studio and by 1784 he had painted 44 of these portraits. His mind was always keen and his interests varied, and in 1786 he decided to make a museum of natural history. He became involved in schemes for America's first scientific museum, and the previous year had formed a society intended to combine an

The Artist in his Museum
*Philadelphia, Acad. of Fine Arts*

59

art school and an exhibition gallery, but the project was split by political tensions. The section led by Peale set up an art school, the first of its kind in America.

As Peale's painting style developed he grew less and less attached to elaboration of form and evolved a simple, precise manner, much in the Neoclassical style of Jacques Louis David in France. In his later years he became absorbed in the study of light and produced canvases of considerable sublety.

*C. C. Sellers   Charles Willson Peale   Philadelphia, 1947*

---

## EDWARD PIERCE                                     died 1695

*A carver in wood and marble*

Little of Edward Pierce's early life is recorded. It is known that he worked as a woodcarver at Wolseley Hall in Staffordshire, and he made fine carvings in the Church of St. Lawrence, Jewry, which was destroyed in 1940. He carried out various commissions for the Guildhall, London, chimney pieces for Castle Bromwich Hall, Warwick, and was employed by Sir Christopher Wren in St. Paul's. Between 1680 and 1681 he helped to build St. Clement Danes Church.

Pierce made a statue of Queen Elizabeth I for the Royal Exchange in 1685, and also one of Edward III. He made busts of famous men, including Milton, Cromwell, and Wren, and between 1689 and 1695 worked at Hampton Court. He died in 1695 after a successful and honored career.

---

## ANTOINE SEBASTIEN PLAMONDON                      1804-1895

*A Canadian portrait painter*

Antoine Sebastien Plamondon was born in 1804 in Ancienne Lorette, Quebec. He had his first art lessons from Joseph Legaré and later assisted his master in restoring the paintings that the Abbé Desjardin had brought to Canada. He went to Paris in 1826 and became a pupil of Paul Guérin, a follower of Jacques Louis David. He traveled also to Venice, Florence, and Rome, making numerous copies of Italian painters.

In 1830 Plamondon returned to Quebec, where he was to become the leading painter of religious scenes and portraits. Technically he was very accomplished and had an uncompromising attitude towards his sitters. He painted some still-lifes, and many altarpieces for churches in and around Quebec. He was commissioned in the 1860's to paint the portrait of Joseph Gauchon, later Lieutenant-Governor of Manitoba, and Plamondon was included in 1864 in a picture of Canadian celebrities. In 1880 he became the first French-Canadian to be admitted to the Royal Canadian Academy. He died in 1895.

*ed. R. H. Hubbard   An Anthology of Canadian Art   Toronto, 1960*

60

## HIRAM POWERS

1805-1873

*An American sculptor of the leaders of his country*

Hiram Powers was born in Vermont. A bust of Lafayette which he cast for a sculptor Frederick Eckstein brought Powers to the notice of the President. In 1835 he went to Washington, where he modeled heads of President Jackson and members of the government. Through the generosity of his friends, Powers emigrated to Florence. In 1837 his villa became the center of a social circle that included the English poets Robert and Elizabeth Browning, and the American Henry Longfellow.

Powers excelled in male portraiture, in which he achieved a smooth strong modeling, dignity, and a feeling for personality. His figures show the influence of Neoclassical ideas. He must also have known the works of Antonio Canova, for such statues as *The Greek Slave*, which caused a sensation at the Great Exhibition in London in 1851, display the same passive idealized beauty.

HIS WORKS INCLUDE
Andrew Jackson
*New York, Met. Mus.*
The Greek Slave, 1846
*Washington, D. C., Corcoran Art Gall.*

**See also page 208**

## SIR HENRY RAEBURN

1756-1823

*A Scottish portrait painter*

Henry Raeburn was apprenticed to a jeweller in about 1772. He began to paint miniature portraits and was so successful that he soon left his master and began to paint full-length portraits for his living.

In 1780 Raeburn married a rich widow and was able to devote himself to painting with no further financial problems. He went to London in 1784, and there met Sir Joshua Reynolds, whose example had influenced his early work. He traveled to Italy, which affected him not at all, and returned to Edinburgh in 1787.

Raeburn soon became the leading painter in Scotland. During the 1790's he developed a fluent, blunt brushwork, ideal for the portrayal of the craggy features of the Scots. While his method of drawing straight on to the canvas with his brush was often successful in conveying the robust personalities of Scots lawyers and lairds, it sometimes betrayed him into insensitivity. He believed that portraits were usually hung rather high, and therefore made a habit of painting his sitter from a low viewpoint.

In 1810 John Hoppner, one of the fashionable London portrait painters, died, and Raeburn went south intending to take over Hoppner's house and practice. Fortunately, he changed his mind, perhaps influenced by Thomas Lawrence's advice and perhaps realizing that his style was not well suited to London taste. He returned to Edinburgh but continued to exhibit regularly at the Royal Academy, visiting London in 1815 when he was elected a member of that institution. In 1822, George IV made a state visit to Edinburgh and crowned Raeburn's many honors by knighting him and appointing him king's limner for Scotland.

*Sir Walter Armstrong   Sir Henry Raeburn   London, 1901*

Lieut. Col. Bryce McMurdo
*London, N. G.*

HIS WORKS INCLUDE
Sir John and Lady Clarke, about 1790
*Rossborough, Ireland, coll. Sir Alfred Beit*
Lady Raeburn, about 1790
*London, coll. the late Countess Mountbatten of Burma*
Lord Newton, about 1803
*London, coll. Earl of Roseberry*
The Macnab, 1819
*London, coll. Messrs. Dewar*

**See also page 117**

Self-portrait
*London, N. P. G.*

*Ramsay*

HIS WORKS INCLUDE

The Macleod of Macleod, 1747
*coll. Dame Flora Macleod of Macleod*

Dr. Mead, 1746
*London, Coram Foundation*

The Painter's Wife, about 1755
*Edinburgh, N. G. of Scotland*

**See also pages 101, 169**

ALLAN RAMSAY                                                    1713-1784

*A major figure in British portraiture*

By 1739 the Edinburgh-born portrait painter Allan Ramsay was settled in London, having undergone a full training in Italy between 1736 and 1738. On his arrival in London his work was found to have a novel air of life and elegance, and he was an immediate success.

During the 1740's Ramsay's only rival in London was Thomas Hudson, and he more than matched Hudson's gift to the Foundling Hospital, a portrait of *Theodore Jacobsen*, with his own gift of *Dr. Mead*, a work in the European Grand Style. In works such as this he achieved the fusion of the Grand Style with English portraiture, which Sir Joshua Reynolds later perfected.

Ramsay's method — a result of his Italian training — was to make a large number of chalk sketches before beginning on the canvas. Many of his sketches show his sensitive touch, particularly in the drawing of hands. Indeed, Ramsay's strength as a painter lay in his sensitivity. He could convey character in terms of color and form, and his contemporary Horace Walpole, when contrasting the style of Ramsay and Reynolds, remarked that "Ramsay was formed to paint women."

Ramsay was never an ambitious man. He was continually busy because of his Scots loyalties, and this sometimes led him to skimp his work and to employ a drapery painter. Even so, he always took the trouble to send studies of posture and costume to his drapery man. The emergence of Reynolds in 1754 prevented him from resting on his laurels, and in 1755 to 1757 he made one of his four journeys to Italy to refresh his eye and memory. His portrait of his wife Margaret, one of his admitted masterpieces, dates from these years. In 1757 he painted the Prince of Wales, and this won him royal patronage. After 1760, however, he seems to have been content with organizing the repetition of royal portraits by assistants. He refused a knighthood, and had no official connection with the Royal Academy. His last years were devoted to literary pursuits.

*A. Smart   The Life and Art of Allan Ramsay   London, 1952*

Lady Catherine Henry
*London, Tate*

The Painter's Wife, about 1755
*Edinburgh, N. G. of Scotland,*

Dr. Mead, 1746
*London, Coram Foundation*

*The founder of academic painting in England*

Joshua Reynolds was born at Plympton in Devon, where his father, a former fellow of an Oxford college, was head of the grammar school. Unlike most painters of his time, therefore, Reynolds came from an educated background and became a man of letters as well as an artist.

Going to London in 1740, Reynolds was apprenticed to the portrait painter Thomas Hudson, but he quickly learned all that Hudson could teach him, and the two amicably parted company after two years. From 1743 to 1749 Reynolds practiced mainly in Devon, although he was in London between 1744 and 1746. In 1746 he painted *The Eliot Family*, a group portrait which is an early example of his habit of making a "classical allusion" in painting, on this occasion to van Dyck.

In 1749 Reynolds sailed for Italy with his friend Commodore Keppel, whose portrait he later painted. This was a vital journey, for Reynolds was able to learn directly from the Italian masters of the Renaissance. He was a scholar by nature and acquired a deep understanding of the Grand Style of portraiture. In Rome from 1750 to 1752, he studied the works of Raphael and Michelangelo. He returned home overland, stopping at Florence, Parma, Bologna, Venice and Paris.

In 1753 Reynolds set up business as a portrait painter in London. He met Dr. Samuel Johnson, and through him all the great literary and intellectual figures of the day, including Oliver Goldsmith, Edmund Burke and David Garrick. A flood of work soon forced him to employ assistants and to make a compromise between the Grand Style he had so much admired in Rome, and the exigencies of "face-painting." At first only Allan Ramsay and Francis Cotes could constitute any sort of rivalry, and by 1768, when the Royal Academy was founded, Reynolds was the only possible choice for president.

Thomas Gainsborough, who arrived in London in 1774, and became Reynolds' first serious rival, said of him "Damn him, how various he is!" This exclamation

Self-portrait, 1780
*London, R. A.*

Heads of Angels (detail) 1787
*London, Tate*

Lord Heathfield, 1787
*London, N. G.*

The Infant Samuel, about 1776
*London, Tate*

Dr. Johnson, about 1770
*London, Tate*

Sir Abraham Hume, about 1783
*London, Tate*

*J Reynolds*

arose from Gainsborough's realization of the wide gamut of expressions and postures at Reynolds' command, his perception of character, and his power to portray all strata of society. Apart from his habit of allusion, Reynolds also liked to introduce symbolic objects into his portraits. So Lord Heathfield, who sat for Reynolds in 1787, carries the keys to the fortress of Gibraltar to show that he was its Governor. In spite of the uneven standard that almost inevitably arises from so large a number of commissions, Reynolds' best works, such as the humorous painting of Garrick and the stern one of Joshua Sharpe, are undeniably great portraits.

Honors continued to be heaped upon him; in 1769 he was knighted and later given academic honors by Oxford, and in 1772 he was made mayor of his birthplace. His most classical and learned works were painted from 1768, suiting his appointment as president of the Academy. From 1769 he delivered fifteen "Discourses" to Academy students. These lectures clearly and sensibly set out the academic viewpoint that it is possible to achieve excellence in art by learning rules and examining the works of one's predecessors.

In 1781 Reynolds made a journey to Flanders and Holland, where the study of Rubens influenced the works of his later years with greater warmth and feeling. After 1789 his failing sight forced him to give up painting, but, according to his many friends, he never lost his cheerful and contented disposition in spite of the painful condition that caused his blindness and, in 1792, his death.

E. K. Waterhouse  Reynolds  London, 1941
D. Hudson  Sir Joshua Reynolds  London. 1958

The Banished Lord
*London, Tate*

HIS WORKS INCLUDE

The Hon. Augustus Keppel, 1753
*Greenwich, London, Nat. Maritime Mus.*

Garrick between Tragedy and
Comedy, about 1761
*England, Private Collection*

Nelly O'Brien, 1763
*London, Wallace Coll.*

Three Ladies Adorning a
Term of Hymen, 1773
*London, N. G.*

**See also pages 104, 105, 106**

64

# GEORGE ROMNEY

*A fashionable portrait painter of the age of Reynolds and Gainsborough*

George Romney was born in Lancashire. Between 1755 and 1757 he was apprenticed to an itinerant portrait painter and afterwards built up a practice in the north of England. In 1762 he moved to London, and the next year won an award from the Society of Arts. After a visit to Paris, Romney established himself in London as the most fashionable portrait painter after Sir Joshua Reynolds.

Although a nervous, unsociable man, Romney was also ambitious, and achieved success through his skill in giving his clients the bloom of youth, good looks, and an air of breeding. He was especially popular because his prices remained lower than those of Reynolds and Gainsborough. Moreover, his portraits did not disturb aristocratic complacency by penetrating the secrets of character. Romney rarely met his sitters outside the studio, and he avoided criticism by refusing to exhibit.

In 1773 Romney abandoned his practice in London to go to Italy for two years. He visited Genoa, writing of the women's dresses that " they produce the most elegant and flowing lines imaginable," a description that recalls his own portraits. The main part of his visit was spent in Rome, where he copied Raphael, and in Venice, studying the works of Titian. His first painting on his return to London, *Mrs. Carwardine and her Son*, showed a new maturity of style which he never bettered.

Romney's style ceased to develop, and his work deteriorated after 1776. He maintained a large clientèle and made a comfortable living producing portraits in strong, clear colors that have survived the passage of time well. In 1781 he met his ideal woman in Emma, Lady Hamilton, but his quasi-historical portraits of her in various stages of dishabille are not among his best works. In response to a longing for the Grand Style he produced hundreds of poor sketches for vast historical scenes. A flicker of his old skill returned with a portrait of *Warren Hastings*, 1795, but in 1798 his health and mind gave way and he returned to his native north of England to die in Kendal in 1802.

*H. Ward and W. Roberts  Romney  London, 1904*

Self-portrait, 1782
*London, N. P. G.*

## HIS WORKS INCLUDE

Mrs. Carwardine and her Son, 1775
*Kelvedon, England, coll. Lord Hillingdon*

The Gower Children, 1771
*coll. Duke of Sutherland*

Sir Christopher and Lady Sykes, 1781
*Sledmere, Yorks, England,
coll. Sir Richard Sykes, Bt.*

Lady Hamilton as a Bacchante,
about 1784
*Kells, Ireland,
coll. Mrs. Tankerville Chamberlayne*

**See also pages 112, 177**

Lady Hamilton
*London, N. G.*

William Cowper, 1792
*London, N. P. G.*

Self-portrait, 1847
*London, N. P. G.*

Mary Magdalene (detail) 1887
*London, Tate*

## HIS WORKS INCLUDE

The Girlhood of Mary Virgin, 1849
*London, Tate*

Paolo and Francesca, 1854
*London, Tate*

Beata Beatrix, about 1863
*London, Tate*

Sancta Lilias, 1874
*London, Tate*

**See also pages 144, 189**

# DANTE GABRIEL ROSSETTI                          1828-1882

*A poet, painter, and founder member of the Pre-Raphaelite Brotherhood*

Dante Gabriel Rossetti was born in London. As a child he steeped himself in romantic literature, wrote poetry, and at 17 began translating Dante. John Sell Cotman taught him drawing and he attended Sass's Academy and the Royal Academy Antique School. In 1848 he begged Ford Madox Brown to accept him as a pupil, but with no master was he patient enough to learn perspective or the technicalities of rendering "pickle jars." About this time he met William Holman Hunt and John Everett Millais, and the three were one in their reaction to Victorian materialism and conventions of painting. From engravings of early Italian masters they saw the simplicity of art before Raphael, and they named their movement the Pre-Raphaelite Brotherhood. In 1849 the first picture to be signed P.R.B. appeared. This was Rossetti's *The Girlhood of Mary Virgin*, for which his sister Christina, the poet, sat, and it accorded with the Brotherhood's ideal of expressing high moral or social ideas painted realistically from nature and individual models.

The Brotherhood was attacked ferociously in the press, and Rossetti, profoundly sensitive to criticism, stopped exhibiting. The individual conceptions of the ideal within the Brotherhood offered no positive counter to official art, and Rossetti himself diverged from the agreed manner. He painted elaborate imaginative detail, idealized his subjects, and used literary themes of medieval romance. His only socially conscious picture, *Found*, was unfinished at his death. The 1850's were Rossetti's best period. Elizabeth Siddall became his most frequent model, and the artist and critic, John Ruskin, was his generous, if exacting patron until 1861. Rossetti used watercolors in a new way, very dry, like oils, in burning, contrasting shades. Elizabeth Siddall, who had become his wife, died in 1862; Rossetti's work declined into a series of single voluptuous female figures, and he employed assistants on details and replicas. In 1869 the publication of his poems was well received, and he was active as a poet until his death. From 1869 to 1871 he painted his last important picture, *Dante's Dream*.

A scandalous and unjust indictment of Rossetti's motives as a poet, together with his constant use of drugs in his last years, undermined his health. He died in London, a virtual recluse, on April 9, 1882.

H. C. Marillier   Dante Gabriel Rossetti   London, 1899
H. R. Angeli   D. G. Rossetti   London, 1949
O. Doughty   A Victorian Romantic, D. G. Rossetti   London, 1949

# LOUIS FRANÇOIS ROUBILIAC                about 1705-1762

*One of the finest sculptors of the 18th century*

Louis François Roubiliac was born in Lyons, and as a youth was apprenticed to Permoser, sculptor to the elector of Saxony. He became an assistant to Nicolas Coustou and won the second Grand Prix in 1730 for a carving of *Daniel Saving Susannah*. In England, two years later, Sir Henry Cheere appointed Roubiliac his assistant.

The statue of Handel for the Vauxhall Pleasure Gardens, 1737, was Roubiliac's first independent commission. Such was its success that he began his own business, making numerous busts and carving church monuments. His second great success came in 1748 with a monument to the Duke of Argyll for Westminster Abbey. Earlier Roubiliac had visited Italy and his *Monument to Lady Elizabeth Nightingale*, 1761, owed much to Bernini's monument to Pope Alexander VII, especially in the symbolic representation of Death.

Roubiliac's sculpture was probably the finest in 18th-century England. It is lively and of superb technique and style; his portrait busts are unsurpassed. For a short time he worked as a modeler for the Chelsea china factory. He died in 1762 and was buried in St. Martin-in-the-Fields.

*K. A. Esdaile  L. F. Roubiliac  Oxford, 1928*

A. CARPENTIERS
Portrait of Louis François Roubiliac
(detail) 1762
*London, N. P. G.*

**HIS WORKS INCLUDE**

Alexander Pope, about 1741
*London, N. P. G.*
Francis Bacon, 1751
*Cambridge, Trinity College*
Shakespeare, 1758
*London, B. M.*

**See also page 201**

---

# THOMAS ROWLANDSON                1756-1827

*A caricaturist of 18th-century England*

Thomas Rowlandson was born in Old Jewry, London, on July 14, 1756, the son of a merchant. By 1759 his father was bankrupt, and he was brought up by his uncle, a silk weaver, and his French Huguenot aunt. In November, 1772, he went to the Royal Academy Schools. In the same year he set out for Paris, where he stayed for two years. Rowlandson was back in London in 1775, for he sent his first drawing to the Academy's annual exhibition in that year, and two years later was awarded the silver medal. Following the first drawing, *Delilah Visiting Samson in Prison*, he exhibited frequently at the Academy.

On inheriting a fortune from his aunt, Rowlandson became extravagant and led a life of dissipation, staying at the gaming table sometimes for 36 hours at a stretch. He soon went through his money, and began to turn to caricature as a means of

Camelford Fair (detail)
*London, Tate*

JOHN JACKSON
Portrait of Thomas Rowlandson
*London, N. P. G.*

*Rowlandson*

67

We Three Logger Heads Be
*Newcastle-upon-Tyne, Laing Art Gall.*

**HIS WORKS INCLUDE**

Doctor Syntax
*New York, Pierpont Morgan Library*
Gaming at Brooks' Club,
about 1810-20
*Kensington Pal., London Mus.*
The Mall, St. James's Park,
about 1815-20
*Kensington Pal., London Mus.*

**See also page 178**

existence. In the 1780's he reached his peak as a watercolorist, and in 1784 he exhibited the drawings, *Vauxhall Gardens* and *Serpentine River*. Three years later he exhibited at the Academy for the last time. The Vauxhall drawing was engraved by Pollard, and the print of it was a great success. In 1788 Rowlandson published *Imitations of Modern Drawings*, consisting of pastiches after Gainsborough, Cipriani and others. Just before this he moved near Carlton House, where George Morland was his neighbor. He was not without patrons, for his work appealed to many among the middle class.

In due course Rowlandson set up a studio with assistants, but his best work was mainly carried out before 1800. He was frequently employed by the art publisher Rudolph Ackerman, who from 1809 to 1811 issued in his "Poetical Magazine" the series of plates, *The Schoolmaster's Tour*, with verses by Dr. William Coombe. These were again engraved by Rowlandson himself in 1812, and issued under the title of *The Tour of Doctor Syntax in Search of the Picturesque*, which was in its fifth edition by 1813. This success was followed up in 1820 by *Doctor Syntax in Search of Consolation*, and in 1821 *The Third Tour of Doctor Syntax in Search of a Wife* appeared. Ackerman also published the *Dance of Death* in 1814-16 and, in 1822, the *Dance of Life*. In addition Rowlandson illustrated works by Smollett, Goldsmith, and Sterne. He drew most of his designs with a reed-pen, with delicate washes of color; they were etched, and aquatinted, and the prints were then colored by hand. In addition to his satires and illustrations, Rowlandson published *A Tour through Wales*, a book based on a journey of 1797, and, with Pugin, *The Microcosm of London*. His fame is due to his numerous drawings, their liveliness, coarseness, and the fact that they depict an astonishing variety of aspects of life in 18th-century England. Rowlandson died in London, after a long illness, on April 22, 1827.

B. Falk   Thomas Rowlandson, his Life And art   London, 1949

---

## WILLIAM RUSH                                                 1756-1833

*The first native-born American sculptor*

William Rush was born and died in Philadelphia, where he at first worked as a carver of ship figureheads between about 1780 and 1790. He served in the Continental Army and came to know George Washington personally, winning the rare distinction of being allowed to draw him from life.

Many of Rush's works are portrait busts. It was his custom to make several plaster replicas of each of his busts and then to paint them to resemble bronze. He never worked in marble, but confined himself to wood and clay, gaining a high reputation for his statues, busts, and ideal figures in these materials. His full-length statue of *George Washington* was originally carved in wood to be the figurehead of a ship of that name. Among the most admired of his ship-carvings were such subjects as the *Genius of the United States*, *Nature*, and *Indian Trader*. His other works include allegorical statues of *Praise* and *Exhortation*, and portrait busts of Linnaeus, William Barton and Lafayette.

**HIS WORKS INCLUDE**

Nymph
*Philadelphia, Acad. of Fine Arts*
Self-portrait
*Philadelphia, Acad. of Fine Arts*
George Washington, 1814
*Philadelphia, Independence Hall*

**See also page 208**

# JOHN RUSKIN                                      1819-1900

*An arbiter of taste in the 19th century*

John Ruskin was strictly brought up in London and well trained in music and drawing. On the continental trips he made with his family he sketched prolifically, but feeling ill suited to being a professional artist he embarked on a literary career. Trained in the classics, he had studied literature at King's College, London, and in 1842 graduated from Christ Church, Oxford. In 1843 his first volume of *Modern Painters* caused a sensation because of its defense of Turner. Ruskin wrote the second volume in Italy, and in 1849 published *The Seven Lamps of Architecture. The Stones of Venice*, 1851, expanded his idea that building and art are an expression of the religion, morality, and habits of a people. He published an essay on the Pre-Raphaelites, whose champion he was to become.

Ruskin became increasingly involved in expounding his views to the public, and his lectures and teaching covered religious and social problems as well as his belief that art is incidental to a more exalted life. He was elected Slade Professor of Art at Oxford in 1869. In 1877 James McNeill Whistler was awarded the famous damages of a farthing in the libel suit he brought against Ruskin.

*P. Quennell  John Ruskin  London, 1949*
*J. Evans  John Ruskin  London, 1954*
*J. Ruskin  The Lamp of Beauty, selections from his writings  London, 1959*

GEORGE RICHMOND
Portrait of John Ruskin
*London, N. P. G.*

## HIS WORKS INCLUDE

Casa Contarini-Fasan, Venice, 1841
*Oxford, Ashmolean*

The Falls of Schaffhausen, 1842
*Cambridge, Mass., Fogg Art Mus.*

The Glacier des Bossons,
Chamonix, 1849
*Oxford, Ashmolean*

**See also page 187**

---

# JOHN MICHAEL RYSBRACK                          1694-1770

*A popular sculptor of the 18th century*

John Michael Rysbrack was the son of a landscape painter and etcher from Antwerp who had worked in England until the hysteria following the Popish Plot made it imperative for him to return to the Continent. Rysbrack was trained under the sculptor Michel van der Voort, but came to England in 1720, and began to work for the architect James Gibbs. Rysbrack gained particular attention with a bust of Lord Nottingham, and afterwards made many busts of historic and contemporary men of note. His success in this line was not challenged until Peter Scheemakers carved a statue of Shakespeare, which was placed in Westminster Abbey. Rysbrack's business thereafter suffered to some extent.

In 1747 Rysbrack began a statue of Hercules, for which he copied various limbs of "the strongest and best made men in London, chiefly the bruisers and boxers." The statue is reputed to have taken him five years to complete. He made various elaborately carved marble chimney pieces for the Duke of Bedford, and a celebrated marble bust of Shakespeare for Alscot Park, Warwickshire. In 1765 Rysbrack retired from business, and died at Vere Street, London, on January 8, 1770.

*M. I. Webb  Michael Rysbrack  London, 1954*

## HIS WORKS INCLUDE

Monument to Sir Isaac Newton, 1731
*London, Westminster Abbey*

John Milton, 1738
*Cambridge, Fitzwm.*

John Locke, 1757
*Oxford, Christ Church College*

**See also page 202**

## PAUL SANDBY

*A sensitive and accurate topographical draftsman*

Paul Sandby was born in Nottingham, and probably taught himself to draw. He was employed as a topographical draftsman by the Duke of Cumberland and was in the Highlands of Scotland with him from 1746 to 1748. Sandby retired from his post in 1752 and settled in London. Many of his drawings of Windsor Castle are in the Windsor Royal Library. He made many watercolor drawings of scenery and architecture, practiced etching, and introduced the aquatint process into England. He published volumes of etchings after his own works and those of other artists.

On several occasions Sandby crossed swords with William Hogarth, the predominant reason being the latter's opposition to the creation of an Academy of Art. He ridiculed Hogarth in cartoons and parodied some of his works. In 1768, when the Royal Academy was founded, Sandby was one of the founder members. He was selected by George III to teach drawing to the young princes, and was drawing master to the Royal Military Academy until 1799. He was among the first watercolor painters to appreciate Welsh scenery. He did not recompose his sketches in the Grand Manner and left many topographically accurate views.

*A. Oppé  Sandby Drawings at Windsor Castle  London, 1947*

Edinburgh Castle, about 1750
*London, Tate*

WILLIAM BEECHEY
Portrait of Paul Sandby (detail)
*London, N. P. G.*

**HIS WORKS INCLUDE**

Fireworks and Illuminations in Green Park on the Occasion of the Peace, October 7, 1748
*London, B. M.*

Somerset House and Garden, 1756
*London, B. M.*

Warwick Castle with the Bridge and Weir, 1775
*London, V. and A.*

Windsor Castle,
the Lower Ward Looking West
*Windsor, Royal Coll.*

**See also page 172**

---

## PETER SCHEEMAKERS

*A Flemish sculptor who found success in England*

Peter Scheemakers was the son of the Antwerp sculptor, Peter Scheemakers the Elder. He worked in Cologne as a journeyman sculptor, but fell ill and found himself in great poverty. Although he was destitute he was determined to reach Rome to study sculpture, and so he walked there. He stayed there only briefly and then traveled to London, where he worked for the sculptors Francis Bird and François (Pierre) Denis Plumière, who also came from Antwerp. At this time Scheemakers

**HIS WORKS INCLUDE**

John Dryden, 1731
*London, Westminster Abbey*

Monument to Charles Fleetwood, 1737
*Ely, England, Cath.*

William Shakespeare, 1741
*London, Westminster Abbey*

Monument to Viscount Howe, 1758
*London, Westminster Abbey*

**See also page 203**

made friends with Laurent Delvaux, and together they executed several works, including the Duke of Buckingham's monument in Westminster Abbey. Scheemakers' most successful work in England was *Shakespeare*, in Westminster Abbey.

In the company of Delvaux, Scheemakers revisited Italy in 1728, and during his stay made careful models. He took these back to England with him as well as several marble statues copied from the antique. From 1747 Scheemakers lived in Vine Street, London, and continued to work there until 1771, when he left England to retire in Antwerp.

---

# SAMUEL SCOTT                                   about 1702-1772

*A marine painter who in later years emulated Canaletto*

So far as is known, Samuel Scott went to sea only once, but all his early works are studies of men-of-war and other craft. One of his earliest known pictures, dated 1729, is of this kind, rather loosely composed and showing sailing vessels lying in a flat calm. In 1732 he joined Hogarth and others on a light-hearted journey from London into Kent, and to the illustrated account of this he contributed a marine view. Scott's finest work in this manner is that commissioned in 1745 by the Earl of Sandwich and Lord Anson, *The Engagement between The Lion and The Elizabeth*.

In 1746 the Venetian painter Canaletto arrived in London, and established a vogue for pictures showing views of the city and reaches of the Thames. By 1748 Scott was exploiting the fashion, but he was by no means a mere imitator of Canaletto. He lacked the Venetian's professional and brilliant finish, but made up for this by a greater understanding of the watery quality of the light and atmosphere of London. Often, as in *The Tower of London*, 1753, he was able to introduce shipping into a view of London, and so to use his old skill. Scott was well paid, and was able to settle comfortably in Twickenham. In 1760 his poor health led him to visit Bath, where he retired in 1765. He died there in 1772, having painted very little in his last years.

*Catalogue of the Scott Exhibition   Guildhall, London, 1955*

The Engagement between The Lion and The Elizabeth (detail) 1745
*London, coll. Lord Sandwich*

HIS WORKS INCLUDE
Views of the East India Settlement, 1732
*London, India Office*
The Tower of London, 1753
*Hambleden, coll. Viscount Hambleden*
Old London Bridge, about 1759
*London, Tate*

**See also page 99**

---

# JOHN SMIBERT                                   1688-1751

*A pioneer of American portraiture*

John Smibert was born in Edinburgh. He trained as an artisan but deciding to become a painter he travelled to London, where he practiced painting quite successfully. He then went to Florence, and there copied many old masters and collected casts of antique sculpture. He met Bishop Berkeley in Italy and was persuaded by him to join a scheme to found a university in Bermuda. Smibert journeyed to America and in 1730 organized an exhibition of his own work in Boston.

HIS WORKS INCLUDE
Bishop Berkeley and His Family, 1729
*New Haven, Conn.,
Yale University Art Gall.*
Mr. and Mrs. William Brown
*Baltimore, John Hopkins University*

**See also page 148**

Smibert had been trained under Sir Godfrey Kneller's influence, and he settled in Boston as a portraitist. His paintings were large competent works, Baroque in character and rich in color. He progressed from a European ideal of elegance to a more realistic style. By about 1749 his eyesight weakened, and for his own amusement he turned to landscape painting. His work influenced John Singleton Copley, and his portraits and his copies of European works laid the foundations of portraiture in New England.

*H. W. Foote   John Smibert, Painter   Harvard, 1950*

---

Self-portrait (detail) about 1848
*London, N. P. G.*

## HIS WORKS INCLUDE

Mrs. Collmann, 1854
*London, Tate*
Monument to the Duke of Wellington, 1856
*London, St. Paul's Cath.*
Study for Mantelpiece in the Saloon at Dorchester House, about 1863
*London, Tate*

**See also page 183**

King Alfred and His Mother (detail) about 1848
*London, Tate*

# ALFRED STEVENS                    1817-1875

*A sculptor, draftsman, and portrait painter*

Alfred Stevens was born in 1817 in Dorset, the son of a painter and decorator. The boy showed an early aptitude for drawing, and a local clergyman lent him engravings to copy. He was later given a little money and a passage to Naples. He spent 18 months in Naples and its environs, making his first contact with Italian painting. In 1835 Stevens walked to Rome, earning a living by drawing portraits, and he then settled in Florence for four years. There he copied works in the Uffizi and produced paintings after various masters for dealers. In 1839 he worked in Venice and Milan, and studied Titian. Two years later he was again in Rome, working with Bertel Thorwaldsen. He returned to England in 1842.

In England, Stevens' ideas were out of keeping with contemporary taste and he was not immediately successful. His first success came with his monument to the Duke of Wellington for St. Paul's Cathedral, though the monument was not set up until 45 years after his death. He worked in various town houses and carved, among other things, caryatids for Dorchester House.

Stevens' many figure drawings, influenced by Raphael, are of a very high quality, and his oil portraits show his humanity and his acute perception. His work became so popular that for many years an entire room was devoted to it at the Tate Gallery.

*K. Towndrow   Alfred Stevens   London, 1939*

# NICHOLAS STONE                                      1586-1647

*A Jacobean monumental mason*

Nicholas Stone was the son of a quarryman, and was born at Woodbury, near Exeter. As a boy he was apprenticed to Isaac James, a London mason. He went to Holland about 1603, and worked under Hendrik de Keyser, a master mason and leading sculptor in Amsterdam, whose daughter Maria he married. Stone is said to have made the portico of the West Church at Amsterdam. He returned to London about 1613 and settled in Southwark. In 1617 he produced the finest of his early works, the tomb of Lady Carey at Stowe-Nine-Churches, Northamptonshire.

In 1619 Stone became Master Mason to James I, and to Charles I on his succession in 1626. He came into contact with the Italianate style of Inigo Jones when he worked under him at the Banqueting House in Whitehall. He worked also at Theobalds and Nonsuch, two royal houses now destroyed. In 1632 he agreed to build a new wing at Cornbury, in Wychwood Forest, for Lord Danby, and he was responsible for the plan of the Goldsmiths' Hall, destroyed in the fire of London.

Stone's monuments were usually distinguished by double-arched canopies, supported by vast console brackets, and pediments within pediments. He discarded some of the conventional designs of the Jacobean monumental sculptors, for instance the four-poster shaped tomb, and the use of obelisks and strapwork ornament. Stone's sons, who died young, were also sculptors. He died on August 24, 1647, in London.

*M. Whinne and O. Millar   English Art, 1625-1714   Oxford, 1957*

Monument to Sir Thomas Bodley, about 1613
*Oxford, Merton College Chapel*

HIS WORKS INCLUDE
Monument to the Earl of Middlesex
*London, Westminster Abbey*
Monument to the
Hon. Francis Holles, 1622
*London, Westminster Abbey*

**See also page 198**

---

# GILBERT STUART                                      1755-1828

*An American portrait painter*

Gilbert Stuart was born in America. He visited Scotland in 1770 and afterwards settled in London. He worked in the studio of Benjamin West but built up a portrait practice of his own. His style shows no imitation of West; rather he must have studied George Romney and John Singleton Copley, whose portrait he painted. This is a work typical of Stuart—a strongly lit, broadly modeled bust set against a romantic sky. To prove wrong those who said he was unable to draw the human form below the waist, Stuart exhibited in 1782 a full length portrait, *Mr. Grant Skating*. This was most successful, but most of Stuart's full lengths are dull, his skill in conveying vitality being almost entirely confined to the face.

Stuart returned to America in 1792. There he paid greater attention to a close likeness and before long he became the most famous of American painters. There are numerous copies of his three portraits of George Washington.

*C. M. Mount   Gilbert Stuart   New York, 1964*

George Washington (detail)
*London, N. P. G.*

HIS WORKS INCLUDE
Mr. Grant Skating, 1782
*Washington, N. G.*
George Washington, 1795
*Boston, Mus. of Fine Arts
Versions may be found in many major
American collections*

**See also page 152**

The Prince of Wales's Phaeton, 1793
*London, Royal Coll.*

## GEORGE STUBBS 1724-1806

*An anatomist and painter of animals*

George Stubbs is unique among artists in that he approached painting through science. While studying anatomy in York as a young man he painted portraits for a living and lectured to medical students.

In 1754 Stubbs visited Rome, despite his declaration that the study of nature is superior to the study of art. Later, in Morocco, he was deeply impressed to see a lion attack a horse and devour it. Back in England he lived in Lincolnshire, dissecting and drawing horses for his work, *The Anatomy of the Horse*. This was published in 1766, by which time he was living in London. All animals, not only horses, interested him, and he made studies of any strange foreign beast that was brought to London.

Stubbs was an artist of an altogether different caliber from the sporting painters of his time. Whatever the animal, his representation of it was invariably accurate. Sometimes his compositions lack unity because of his practice of building the landscape around the animal, but his works have great charm, his subordination of men to horses being less naïve than at first it seems. Most of his work is oil on canvas, although from 1778 he was painting with enamel on copper and china for Josiah Wedgwood.

The Prince of Wales favored Stubbs with his patronage during the 1790's and one of the finest works to come out of this association was *The Prince of Wales's Phaeton*, painted in 1793. Stubbs continued to paint and dissect enthusiastically until the end of his long and vigorous life in 1806.

*B. Taylor  Catalogue of the Stubbs Exhibition  Walker Art Gallery, Liverpool, 1951*

**HIS WORKS INCLUDE**

A Horse Frightened by a Lion, 1770
*Liverpool, England, Walker Art Gall.*
The Prince of Wales's Phaeton, 1793
*London, Royal Coll.*
Hambletonian Rubbing Down, 1800
*Liverpool, England, Walker Art Gall.*

**See also pages 107, 179**

## PIETRO TORRIGIANO 1472-1528

*A Florentine sculptor employed by English kings*

Pietro Torrigiano was one of several young artists who studied in the school founded by Lorenzo the Magnificent in Florence. He later worked in Rome, helping Pinturicchio in modeling the stucco decorations in the Borgia Apartment.

He was invited to England to execute the magnificent bronze tomb of Henry VII and his queen in Westminster Abbey. The tomb, finished in 1517, is his acknowledged masterpiece. The tomb of Henry VII's mother, Margaret of Richmond, was probably also made by Torrigiano. The altar, retable, and baldachin commissioned to stand before Henry's tomb were destroyed in the 17th century, likewise the uncompleted bronze tomb for Henry VIII. Torrigiano died in Spain in 1528.

*J. Lees-Milne  Tudor Renaissance  London, 1951*

**HIS WORKS INCLUDE**

Tomb of Lady Margaret Beaufort,
Countess of Richmond and Derby,
1509
*London, Westminster Abbey*
Tomb of Henry VII
and Margaret of York, 1509-17
*London, Westminster Abbey*

**See also page 193**

# JOHN TRUMBULL

*A heroic painter of great talent who never had the chance to fulfil his potentialities*

John Trumbull was born in Connecticut, and showed an early aptitude for drawing, but he was not encouraged in this by his family. For some time he experimented with portrait painting, using home-made materials, and in 1784 he went to London to study with Benjamin West.

Trumbull returned to America and served as aide-de-camp to George Washington. His army days inspired him to paint scenes of the most important episodes of the Revolution. When he went back to London in 1789 he took some sketches, and fully expected that engravings after his pictures could be sold at considerable profit. Unfortunately there was little lasting enthusiasm for his prints. Trumbull accepted a diplomatic post in London in 1794, and gave up painting for a time. He remained in London when his post terminated, and took up the profession of portrait painter with only moderate success.

In America, Trumbull was commissioned to execute four Revolution scenes for the decoration of the rotunda of the Capitol. Even in this his luck was only partial, for years of discouragement had blunted his enthusiasm, and the scenes chosen were not those most satisfying pictorially. His work was imposing and dignified, but also tended to be flat and lifeless. In general these paintings were coolly received and the four remaining panels were not given to Trumbull.

In 1817 Trumbull became head of the American Academy of Fine Arts in New York, which incorporated a gallery and an art school. His naturally distrustful nature and his many disappointments had made him soured and unpleasant. He ruined the gallery by selling it his own works at exorbitant prices, and he suppressed all signs of individuality among the students, eventually causing the Academy to split and lose its importance. He died in 1843.

T. Sizer  *The Works of John Trumbull, Artist of the American Revolution*  Yale, 1950
ed. T. Sizer  *Autobiography of Col. John Trumbull*  Yale, 1953

SAMUEL LOVETT WALDO
Portrait of John Trumbull (detail)
*New Haven, Conn.,*
*Yale University Art Gall.*

HIS WORKS INCLUDE
Priam Returning with the
Body of Hector, 1785
*Boston, Atheneum*
The Death of General Montgomery
at Quebec, 1786
*New Haven, Conn.,*
*Yale University Art Gall.*
The Capture of the Hessians at
Trenton, 1786-97
*New Haven, Conn.,*
*Yale University Art Gall.*
Sortie of the British Garrison
from Gibraltar, 1789
*Boston, Atheneum*

**See also page 153**

The Death of General Montgomery
at Quebec, 1786
*New Haven, Conn.,*
*Yale University Art Gall.*

The Declaration of Independence
(detail) begun 1789
*New Haven, Conn.,*
*Yale University Art Gall.*

Self-portrait, 1792
*London, N. P. G.*

## HIS WORKS INCLUDE

Frosty Morning, 1813
*London, N. G.*
Boccaccio Relating the Tale
of the Birdcage, about 1823
*London, Tate*
Stormy Sea, late period
*London, Tate*
There is a large Turner collection
in the Tate Gallery, London.

**See also pages 126, 127, 128, 186**

# JOSEPH MALLORD WILLIAM TURNER 1775-1851

*A great precursor of the Impressionists*

Joseph Mallord William Turner was born on April 23, 1775, in Maiden Lane, Covent Garden, where his father had been established for some years as a barber. When he was a child, he stayed in Brentford for four years, while recovering from some illness. He lived there with his uncle, and went to Brentford Free School, though he proved to have little ability for learning. At this time he began to copy any landscape engravings he could find. He was determined to become an artist, and in 1789 he was admitted to the Royal Academy Schools, where he probably studied under Thomas Malton. He drew from the antique, and also made landscape studies, showing even at this stage a natural feeling for form.

In 1791 Turner exhibited at the Academy for the first time, when he showed two watercolors at the Annual Exhibition. After the exhibition he went to the country to make drawings and sketches and in the following years he explored many parts of Britain, going most frequently to the south country, to Wales, and the north of England, though he also visited Scotland and Lincolnshire. Turner in the early years of his career did not show great originality. He copied many drawings made by accepted contemporary painters, and for some time was strongly influenced by Thomas Girtin, to whose watercolors some of his own works were very close. He and Girtin worked together for three years in the mid-1790's at Dr. Thomas Monro's house, copying works by John Cozens. This proved good training for Turner, who absorbed Cozens' strong sense of composition.

From 1791 Turner exhibited at the Royal Academy regularly until the last years of his life. The Academy provided him with much support against the critics who misunderstood his work, and against the arbiters of contemporary aristocratic taste, who found that his paintings lacked finish. The most persistent of his opponents was Sir George Beaumont, who adversely affected his sale of oil paintings. For most of his life Turner's main source of income was from his watercolors, and engravings made from them. In 1799 he was elected an associate of the Academy; in 1802 he became a member, and in 1807 professor of perspective—a post that he fulfilled only erratically, and from which he resigned in 1836. In 1845 he became deputy president.

The Shipwreck (detail) 1805
*London, Tate*

Calais Pier: an English Packet
Arriving (detail) about 1803
*London, Tate*

Turner worked only in watercolor until about 1796; in this year he probably exhibited his first oil painting. In 1803 he decided to build his own gallery, partly because of internal quarrels in the Academy, and partly because both his output and the demand for his work were increasing. This also enabled him to have greater independence of prejudiced criticism. The painters who exerted most influence on him were Claude, Richard Wilson, the Dutch 17th-century marine painters, and Rubens. Turner also admired Poussin, though he absorbed few elements of his style.

Venice (detail) 1833
*London, Tate*

Besides making sketching trips in Britain, Turner visited the Continent frequently. His first journey abroad was to France, to visit the collection of works of art made by Napoleon on his campaigns, and Switzerland, in 1802. He returned on several occasions and the sketches he made were used later as a basis for paintings. In 1819 he went to Italy, on the suggestion of Lawrence, and although his first drawings there were primarily architectural, his palette from this time became lighter and more brilliant, matching that of his watercolors, and his interest in light developed. His vision had become intensely personal, and he had moved from a stormy, Romantic style to an interest in the more subtle renderings of light and atmosphere. Turner returned to Italy in 1828, and to Venice seven years later, and again in 1840, by which time he had evolved a method of painting that provides some parallel with Impressionism. The later views of Venice are ethereal yet brilliant in color.

In the later years of his life Turner produced remarkable effects of atmosphere

The Fighting Téméraire, 1838
*London, N. G.*

The Pass of St. Gothard, about 1814
*Birmingham, England, City Art Gall.*

and light, particularly in *The Fighting Téméraire*, 1838, the *Snowstorm*, 1842, and *Rain, Steam and Speed*, 1844, the last important oil painting exhibited by him. In these years his work had gone rather out of favor. The young John Ruskin brought him once more to the public notice in his *Modern Painters*, published in 1843. Turner had always been solitary by nature; in his last years, when he was ill and depressed, this tendency increased. He retired to a cottage in Chelsea, where he could watch the river, and there he died, on December 19, 1851.

Between 1807 and 1819 Turner was engrossed in producing a series of engravings to be published as the *Liber Studiorum*. For these he made drawings in sepia or bistre of different kinds of landscapes. Originally a hundred plates were planned, but lack of public support and Turner's own parsimony prevented any real success of this venture. Thomas Lawrence described Turner as "indisputably the finest landscape painter in Europe." Turner, through an individual technique, arrived at results that to some extent foreshadow Impressionism, but he did not paint directly from nature.

*A. J. Finberg   J. M. W. Turner (revised edition)   Oxford, 1961*
*M. Butlin   Turner Watercolors   London, 1962*

---

Hope, 1885
*London, Tate*

**HIS WORKS INCLUDE**

Lady Castletown, 1846
*London, Tate*

Hope, 1885
*London, Tate*

Eve Tempted, about 1896
*London, Tate*

Lord Tennyson, 1895
*London, N. P. G.*

**See also page 140**

## GEORGE FREDERIC WATTS      1817-1904

*A painter of portraits and allegorical scenes*

George Frederic Watts was born in London. In 1835 he was admitted to the Royal Academy Schools, where he showed great promise. He then took a studio and gained several commissions, and he exhibited a painting at the Academy. A competition for the decoration of the new Houses of Parliament was held in 1843; Watts entered a drawing, *Caractacus Being Led in Chains through Rome*, and won second prize.

With his prize money, Watts went to Italy. In Florence he taught drawing to the daughters of Lady Duff Gordon until an attachment developed between him and one of the daughters, Georgina. He turned to his painting with renewed vigor when the family returned to Rome. In 1847 Watts returned to England to enter a competition for decorating the House of Lords. His *Alfred Inviting the Saxons to Resist the Landing of the Danes* won first prize, and similar commissions followed, including *St. George Overcomes the Dragon* for the Houses of Parliament. His dream of decorating a large hall with a complex scheme representing history and civilization never materialized and he was forced to earn a living by portrait painting. He painted many eminent men, including Tennyson and Thiers, but he gradually became disillusioned.

In 1867 Watts became a member of the Royal Academy. He turned increasingly to allegorical subjects and also experimented with sculpture. *Clytie*, 1868, is a vigorous example. He held several exhibitions, including ones in Paris and the United States, and built his own gallery. He married for the second time in 1886, and his life was from then on run by his wife, who took a passionate interest in his work. He died in 1904. Watts was sincere in his desire to be uplifting, but if he could have distinguished sentiment from sentimentality he would have been a finer artist.

*M. S. Watts  G. F. Watts  London, 1912*
*D. Loshak  Catalogue of the Watts Exhibition  Tate Gallery, London, 1954*

---

# BENJAMIN WEST                                               1738-1820

*An American who began a new kind of painting in England*

Benjamin West came of Pennsylvania Quaker stock, and first learned to paint in America. In 1760 he travelled to Italy, where he spent three years in Rome, Florence, Bologna, and Venice, enjoying everywhere the prestigious novelty of being an American. The blind cardinal, Albani, asked him if he were not a Red Indian, and he was generally considered to be a rarity. In Rome he was drawn into the circle of the German Neoclassical painter Anton Raffael Mengs and the art historian Johann Winckelmann.

In 1763 West set himself up in London as a portrait painter, and became a founder member of the Royal Academy in 1768. Influenced by the Neoclassical style, he began to paint history pictures on a small scale, and it was as a historical painter that he became really successful. Archbishop Drummond, who commissioned him to paint *Agrippina Landing at Brindisi*, introduced him to George III in 1768. This was to be for West a long and profitable association, starting with *The Final Departure of Regulus from Rome*, commissioned by the king and shown at the Academy in 1769. Such works exactly suited the king's taste by their very limitations and their somewhat prosaic qualities, and they also became popular through engravings.

West's greatest success came in 1771. In this year he painted *The Death of Wolfe*, the first attempt to commemorate a contemporary event in contemporary dress. Strange as it seems today, it had been the usual custom to paint such events in classical costume. Even so, West made no attempt to make his work historically accurate, and the composition of the figures is in the tradition of a thousand depictions of the Deposition. So popular was the work that the engravings brought West £15,000.

Later, West turned to the representation of medieval subjects in medieval dress; again, he was the first to try this sort of subject and again he was successful. In 1792 he succeeded Sir Joshua Reynolds as president of the Royal Academy, but refused a knighthood because of his Quaker principles. West had little feeling for color or for the texture of paint, and his direct influence on English painting was small. His real importance in the history of art is to be found among the French artists of the Revolutionary and Napoleonic eras, for whom he established a precedent for the painting of contemporary history.

*J. Galt  Life and Works of Benjamin West  London, 1820*

GILBERT STUART
Portrait of Benjamin West
*London, N. P. G.*

## HIS WORKS INCLUDE

Departure of Regulus, 1769
*Kensington Pal., London Mus.*

Death of Wolfe, 1771
*Kensington Pal., London Mus.*
*and Ottawa, N. G. of Canada*

St. Paul Shaking off the Viper, 1786
*London, Greenwich Hospital*

Death on the Pale Horse, 1817
*Philadelphia, Acad. of Fine Arts*

**See also page 114**

# FRANCIS WHEATLEY 1747-1801

Self-portrait
*London, N. P. G.*

*F. Wheatley*

HIS WORKS INCLUDE

The Irish House of Commons, 1780
*coll. Mrs. G. Gascoigne*
Mr Howard Relieving Prisoners, 1787
*Sandon, coll. Earl of Harrowby*

**See also page 115**

*A painter of portraits and genre subjects*

Francis Wheatley, who may have been a pupil of Johann Zoffany, began as a painter of small portraits and conversation pieces. Such works made up his early exhibits at the Society of Artists from 1765. From 1779 to 1783 or 1784 Wheatley lived and worked in Dublin, building up a considerable reputation. The most famous work of his Dublin years, a mass portrait of the Irish House of Commons, clearly shows his debt to Zoffany, but in other paintings he reveals a broader feeling for landscape than Zoffany ever achieved.

On his return to London Wheatley gave up group portraits to paint genre subjects such as Greuze was making popular in France—subjects which placed emphasis on the picturesque and virtuous qualities of the poor. *Mr. Howard Relieving Prisoners*, painted in 1787, plays upon the moral feelings of the spectator, while the *Cries of London* series, engraved in 1795, exploits his sense of the picturesque. It was upon the engraving of these works, particularly the popular *Cries*, that Wheatley's income chiefly depended. In spite of their concessions to sentimentality, these works are not unworthy, for they show a free, sensitive touch and a sense of color. One small full-length portrait of 1786, *Arthur Philip*, depicts the first governor of New South Wales walking on a beach. With its broad effects, clean outline, and clear color, it reveals the best of Wheatley's capabilities.

W. Roberts  *F. Wheatley, R. A.  London, 1910*

---

# SIR DAVID WILKIE 1785-1841

Self-portrait
*Edinburgh, Nat. Gall. of Scotland*

*An artist beloved for his homely genre subjects*

David Wilkie was the son of a Fifeshire minister and from the age of 14 spent four years in The Trustees' Academy, Edinburgh, where he studied the etchings and engravings of Rembrandt and Adriaen van Ostade. In 1805 he entered the Academy Schools in London, and the following year exhibited a painting entitled *Village Politicians*. This anecdotal work made his name, and he continued to treat similar subjects in a similar way for some 20 years. These scenes from village life, which are studies in character rather than moral tales, are in the tradition of Teniers and Hogarth. The small figures, for example in *Blind Man's Buff*, are pointed and witty in pose and gesture. Both as an artist and in society, Wilkie displayed a charming sincerity which made his gaucheries endearing.

In 1824 a series of family misfortunes broke down Wilkie's health, and he went abroad for three years to recuperate. He returned with seven pictures of Spanish and Italian subjects, which he exhibited at the Academy in 1829. These show a change in subject matter and style. The design is firmer and the scale of the figures larger, but the acute observation of the early peasant scenes has been lost. Wilkie painted also some large historical canvases, such as *Sir David Baird Discovering the*

*Body of Tippoo Sahib*, a successful Baroque composition. Generally, these works were not approved of, although he continued to be honored and respected. In 1840 Wilkie made a journey to the Holy Land, and from there he went to Alexandria, where he painted a small brilliant portrait of Mohammed Ali. This was his last work, for he fell ill on the journey home, and died soon after his ship left Malta. His burial at sea was the subject of a famous painting by Turner, and he was mourned by the whole nation.

A. Cunningham   *Life of Sir David Wilkie*   London, *1943*
J. Woodward   *Catalogue of the Wilkie Exhibition*   Royal Academy, London, *1958*

The Penny Wedding, 1819
*London, Royal Coll.*

**HIS WORKS INCLUDE**

The Blind Fiddler, 1806
*London, Tate*
The Penny Wedding, 1819
*London, Royal Coll.*
The Maid of Saragossa, 1828
*London, Royal Coll.*
Sir David Baird Discovering the Body of Tippoo Sahib, 1839
*Edinburgh, Castle*

**See also pages 134, 182**

---

## RICHARD WILSON                                    1713-1782

*A Welsh landscape painter of classical inclination*

As the son of a Welsh clergyman, Richard Wilson was given a sound classical education, and his landscape painting shows the classical overtones of Claude, Nicolas Poussin, and Gaspard Poussin. These three painters and Albrecht Cuyp were his acknowledged masters. Wilson was first apprenticed to a portrait painter in London but, although accomplished, he was temperamentally unsuited to fashionable portraiture, and as early as 1746 he turned to landscapes, painting two small circular views of London for the Foundling Hospital.

It was while Wilson was in Rome between 1752 and 1757 that he finally decided to concentrate on landscape painting. He wandered over the Campagna making small memorandum sketches, most of which he used after his return to England. Only a few large canvases belong to his Italian years, while nearly half his output after his return to England was of Italian scenes. The merit of his work was always recognized by his fellow artists but rarely by the public. His work in England falls into roughly three categories. First there were his Italian views, some of which, *Niobe* for instance, were mythological history paintings, and some simply contained unidentified pastoral personalities. Second, there were the English and Welsh landscapes that were his most original contribution to English art. Last, he painted commissioned views of English country houses. These were his only

Richard Wilson
after a portrait by R.A. Mengs
*London, N. P. G.*

works that were consistently profitable and, far from being mere pot-boilers, they are among the finest of their sort. In spite of his great industry Wilson was never able to make more than a meager living by his art. He eventually retired to North Wales, an impoverished and broken man.

Once Wilson's style had been formed, it changed little. He often repeated a successful composition many times, but usually with changes in detail. His best works, such as *Snowdon from Llyn Nantlle*, show a pure classicism that is in strong contrast to John Constable's naturalism and which made Wilson the greatest English exponent of the Grand Manner in landscape painting.

B. Ford   *Drawings of Richard Wilson*   London, 1951
W. G. Constable   *Richard Wilson*   London, 1953

The Destruction of Niobe's Children
*Formerly London, Tate (destroyed World War II)*

Snowdon from Llyn Nantlle, about 1765-75
*Liverpool, England, Walker Art Gall.*

## JOSEPH WILTON                                                    1722-1803

*A sculptor and decorator*

Joseph Wilton studied under Jean Baptiste Pigalle in Paris and was trained to work in marble. He traveled to Rome in 1747 with Louis Roubiliac, and there won the Jubilee gold medal awarded by Pope Benedict XIV. For four years he settled in Florence and manufactured many marble copies of antique statues.

Wilton returned to his native England in 1755 and in 1758 was appointed with the decorative painter Cipriani director of the gallery of painting and sculpture at Whitehall. He was also appointed sculptor to George III in 1764, having previously made some of the designs and carvings for the state coach. Wilton had many commissions for decorations at Somerset House, and for the Royal Academy, including four huge statues, 1778, entitled *Europe, Asia, Africa,* and *America.* He made ornamented chimney pieces for Blenheim House and other country seats, and executed varied decorative works. There are several statues of George III by Wilton, and also of William Pitt. He was a founder member of the Royal Academy, and in 1790 he was appointed keeper of the Royal Academy.

# THOMAS WOOLNER

1825-1892

*A Pre-Raphaelite sculptor*

Thomas Woolner was born in Suffolk, later moving to London with his family. He became a pupil of the sculptor, Henry Behnes, and then of Henry's brother William, subsequently attending the Royal Academy Schools. *Eleanor Sucking Poison from Prince Edward's Wounds*, 1843, was his first exhibited group, followed by *Boadicea*, 1844, at Westminster Hall. In 1848 he became one of the Pre-Raphaelite Brotherhood. He began to model medallion portraits, but these had only a slight success, and it was not until he returned from an unprofitable venture in Australia that his reputation became established with his bust of Tennyson and portrait medallion of Carlyle. In the following years he made busts and monuments of various eminent men. He exhibited at the Royal Academy and was appointed professor of sculpture in 1877. He died in 1892.

*A. Woolner   Thomas Woolner, Life and Letters   London, 1917*
*T. S. R. Boase   English Art, 1800-1870   Oxford, 1959*

### HIS WORKS INCLUDE

Richard Cobden, 1865
*London, Westminster Abbey*
Lord Macaulay, 1866
*Cambridge, Trinity College Chapel*
Lord Palmerston, 1876
*London, Parliament Square*
Monument to Sir Edwin Landseer, 1882
*London, St. Paul's Cath.*

**See also page 208**

---

# JOSEPH WRIGHT

1734-1797

*A portrait painter and recorder of scenes by artificial light*

Joseph Wright was the son of an attorney in the Midland town of Derby, where he at first intended to become an engineer. His father, however, encouraged his liking for art, and in 1751 sent him to London, where he worked for two years in the studio of the fashionable portrait painter Thomas Hudson.

In 1753 Wright returned to his home town and practiced there, later working under Hudson for another period of fifteen months because he felt his knowledge to be deficient. After this he began to build a reputation as a portrait painter in Derby, and also painted some industrial and scientific subjects, such as *A Philosopher Giving a Lecture on the Orrery*, and *An Iron Forge*, painted in 1772. These two are examples of his liking for scenes lit by candle or fire.

In 1773 Wright made the conventional journey to Italy, but though he painted some Italian subjects, often based on a memorable eruption of Vesuvius that he saw, the journey had no effect on his style. On his return to London Wright made an attempt to replace Gainsborough in Bath, but after two disastrous years he wisely returned to Derby, where his less elegant clients welcomed his realistic style. He became an associate of the Royal Academy in 1781, but soon had the usual quarrel with the Academy over the hanging of his pictures, which were sometimes placed so low as to be on a level with the feet of the spectator. He was eventually elected a full member in 1784, but his association with the Academy was never a happy one. Although often encouraged to try his fortunes in London, Wright remained in Derby until his death in 1797.

*W. Bemrose   Joseph Wright, A.R.A.   London, 1885*
*B. Nicolson   Catalogue of the Wright of Derby Exhibition   Tate, London, 1953*

Self-portrait (detail)
*London, N. P. G.*

### HIS WORKS INCLUDE

A Philosopher Giving a Lecture on the Orrery, about 1765
*Derby, England, Mus. and Art Gall.*
Experiment with the Air-pump, about 1768
*London, Tate*
An Iron Forge, 1772
*London, coll. the late Countess Mountbatten of Burma*

**See also page 111**

## MICHAEL WRIGHT

1617-1700

*A portrait painter whose success was overshadowed by his great contemporaries*

Tradition has it that Michael Wright was a Scot, but it is possible that he was the Michael Wright baptized in London in May, 1617. He went to Italy in about 1647, but because of his antiquarian interests he learned less there than he might have. Nicolas Poussin and Velázquez were painting in Rome at the time, but Wright was intent upon his collection of gems, coins, and shells. He returned to England in 1656 and painted Mrs. Claypole, Cromwell's daughter, in the Italianate style he had adopted. After the Restoration he made no attempt to adapt his style to court taste, so that although he had some court commissions he inevitably remained second to Sir Peter Lely. It is possible, from the existence of several Scottish portraits, that he visited Scotland between 1662 and 1665.

Between 1671 and 1675 Wright painted 22 portraits of civic dignitaries, but these are heavily restored. In 1685 he went to Rome as steward of the Earl of Castlemaine. Wright wrote an account of the journey but did no painting in Rome or after his return. Although Lely was by this time dead, Wright's absence left the way open for the brilliant young Godfrey Kneller. Wright had been more sensitive to character than Lely, but he was not successful. He was forced to sell his books and collections, and died in 1700. He is buried in St. Paul's Church, Covent Garden.

*E. K. Waterhouse   Painting in Britain, 1530-1790   London, 1953*

A Highland Chieftain (detail)
about 1680
*Glasgow, City Art Gall.*

### HIS WORKS INCLUDE

Mrs. Claypole, 1658
*London, N. P. G.*
Colonel John Russell, 1659
*Richmond, Surrey· England, Ham House*
Charles II
*London, Royal Coll.*

**See also page 92**

---

## JOHANN ZOFFANY

1734/5-1810

*A genre painter whose theater scenes won him popularity*

Johann Zoffany was born in Frankfurt, the son of a Bohemian Jew from Prague Soon after 1760, Zoffany was in London, where he was at first forced by poverty to paint draperies. He was rescued from this by David Garrick, the actor, who saw the publicity value of pictures of himself and his company. As a result Zoffany painted theatrical scenes, such as *Garrick in "The Farmer's Return,"* his best work.

Theatrical groups led naturally to conversation pieces, and one of Zoffany's most accomplished, entitled *Queen Charlotte and her Two Eldest Children*, shows the king's family in about 1766. It is unexcelled in its minute imitation of nature. In 1772 Zoffany went to Florence, probably at the king's expense, and there painted *The Tribune of the Uffizi.*

Zoffany returned to England in 1779, only to find that the fashion for his work had passed. In 1783 he went to India, where he prospered, but he grew increasingly indifferent to the intellectual aspect of painting, relying purely on his technique. Although he would never have been a great painter, Zoffany was to some extent the victim of the success he achieved when his youthful works established him as the creator and master of theatrical painting.

*Lady Victoria Manners and G. C. Williamson   John Zoffany, R.A,   London, 1920*

### HIS WORKS INCLUDE

Garrick in
"The Farmer's Return", 1762
*Durham, England, coll. Earl of Durham*
The Tribune of the Uffizi
*London, Royal Coll.*
A Scene from
"The Clandestine Marriage"
*London, Garrick Club*
The Sharp Family Making Music
on the Thames at Fulham
*Gloucestershire, England,
coll. Miss Olive Lloyd-Baker*

**See also page 113**

# Color
# Plates

## 1 BRITISH

GERLACH FLICKE  Portrait of an Unknown Nobleman, 1547  *oil on wood  39½ × 29½ in.*
*Edinburgh, National Gallery of Scotland*

HANS EWORTH  Lady Dacre, about 1554  *oil on wood*  *29 × 22¾ in.*
*Ottawa, National Gallery of Canada*

NICHOLAS HILLIARD   A Youth Leaning against a Tree among Roses
about 1588   *watercolor on vellum*   $5\frac{3}{8} \times 2\frac{3}{4}$ *in.*
*London, Victoria and Albert Museum*

ISAAC OLIVER  An Unknown Lady, about 1605  *watercolor  diameter 5 in.*
*Cambridge, England, Fitzwilliam Museum*

DANIEL MYTENS  The 1st Duke of Hamilton, 1629  *oil on canvas*  *85 × 53½ in.*
*Edinburgh, National Gallery of Scotland, collection the Duke of Hamilton*

SAMUEL COOPER Oliver Cromwell, 1657  watercolor  $3\frac{1}{4} \times 2\frac{1}{2}$ in.
Drumlanrig Castle, Scotland, collection the Duke of Buccleuch and Queensberry

WILLIAM DOBSON   The Artist, Sir Charles Cotterell and Sir Balthasar Gerbier, about 1645   *oil on canvas   38¼ × 49¼ in.*
*Albury Park, Guildford, England, collection Helen, Duchess of Northumberland*

MICHAEL WRIGHT  Mrs. Claypole, 1658  *oil on canvas  21 × 17¼ in.*
*London, National Portrait Gallery*

SIR PETER LELY  Sir Frescheville Holles and Sir Robert Holmes, about 1670  *oil on canvas  52 × 64 in.*
*London, National Maritime Museum*

SIR GODFREY KNELLER   Sir Isaac Newton, 1702   *oil on canvas*   *30 × 25 in.*
*London, National Portrait Gallery*

JOSEPH HIGHMORE  Pamela Tells a Nursery Story, about 1744  *oil on canvas  25 × 31 in.*
*Cambridge, England, Fitzwilliam Museum*

WILLIAM HOGARTH   Marriage à la Mode, scene ii, 1743   *oil on canvas*   *27 × 35 in.*
*London, National Gallery*

WILLIAM HOGARTH  The Wanstead Assembly  *oil on canvas*  *25 × 30¼ in.*
*South London Art Gallery, Camberwell Borough Council*

WILLIAM HOGARTH  The Painter and his Pug, 1745  *oil on canvas*  $35\frac{1}{2} \times 27\frac{1}{2}$ *in.*
*London, Tate Gallery*

SAMUEL SCOTT   Part of Old Westminster Bridge   *oil on canvas*   $10\frac{3}{4} \times 15\frac{1}{2}$ *in.*
*London, Tate Gallery*

ARTHUR DEVIS  Mr. and Mrs. William Atherton, about 1747  *oil on canvas  36 × 50 in.*
*Liverpool, England, Walker Art Gallery*

ALLAN RAMSAY  Mrs. Martin, 1761  *oil on canvas   50 × 40 in.*
*Birmingham, England, City Museum and Art Gallery*

RICHARD WILSON  Lake Albano and Castel Gandolfo, 1754  *oil on canvas  30 × 39¼ in.*
*Port Sunlight, Cheshire, England, Lady Lever Art Gallery*

RICHARD WILSON   Valley of the Mawddach   *oil on canvas*   *39¾ × 42 in.*
*Liverpool, England, Walker Art Gallery*

SIR JOSHUA REYNOLDS  Nelly O'Brien, 1762  *oil on canvas*  $49\frac{3}{4} \times 39\frac{1}{4}$ *in.*
*London, Wallace Collection*

SIR JOSHUA REYNOLDS  Garrick between Tragedy and Comedy, about 1761  *oil on canvas*  *58×72 in.*
*England, Private Collection*

SIR JOSHUA REYNOLDS   Colonel St. Leger, 1778   *oil on canvas   93 × 58 in.*
*Waddesdon Manor, Aylesbury, England, National Trust*

GEORGE STUBBS   Mares and Foals in a Landscape, about 1760-69   *oil on canvas   40 × 63¾ in.*
*London, Tate Gallery*

THOMAS GAINSBOROUGH   Mr. and Mrs. Andrews, about 1750   *oil on canvas*   $27\frac{1}{2} \times 47$ *in.*
*London, National Gallery*

THOMAS GAINSBOROUGH  Mary, Countess Howe, about 1760
*oil on canvas  96×60 in.*
*London, Kenwood, Iveagh Bequest*

THOMAS GAINSBOROUGH  The Harvest Wagon, about 1767   *oil on canvas*   *47½ × 57 in.*
*Birmingham, England, Barber Institute of Fine Arts*

JOSEPH WRIGHT   Experiment with the Air-pump, about 1768   *oil on canvas*   *72×96 in.*
*London, Tate Gallery*

GEORGE ROMNEY   Lady Hamilton in a Straw Hat, about 1785   *oil on canvas   29¼ × 24¼ in.*
*San Marino, California,   Henry E. Huntington Art Gallery*

JOHANN ZOFFANY   The Dutton Family, about 1765   *oil on canvas*   *40 × 50½ in.*
*Farley Hall, Reading, England, collection the Hon. Peter Samuel*

BENJAMIN WEST  The Death of Wolfe, 1771   *oil on canvas   59½ × 84 in.*
*Ottawa, National Gallery of Canada*

FRANCIS WHEATLEY  Lord Aldeburgh Reviewing Troops, 1782  *oil on canvas*  $61 \times 94\frac{1}{2}$ *in.*
*Waddesdon Manor, Aylesbury, England, National Trust*

JOHN ROBERT COZENS  Gardens of the Villa Negroni, 1783  *watercolor  $11\frac{1}{4} \times 15$ in.*
*England, collection Commander H. L. Agnew*

SIR HENRY RAEBURN   Mrs. Colin Campbell of Park   *oil on canvas   30 × 25 in.*
*Glasgow, Art Gallery and Museum*

HENRY FUSELI  Macbeth and the Witches  *oil on canvas  66 × 53 in.*
*Petworth House, Sussex, England, Petworth Collection*

**WILLIAM BLAKE** The Whirlwind of Lovers, about 1824 *pen and ink with watercolor* $14\frac{3}{4} \times 20\frac{7}{8}$ *in.*
*Birmingham, England, City Museum and Art Gallery*

GEORGE MORLAND   The Ale House Door, 1792   *oil on canvas*   $24\frac{3}{4} \times 30$ *in.*
*Edinburgh, National Gallery of Scotland*

BENJAMIN MARSHALL   Francis Dukinfield Astley and his Harriers, 1809   *oil on canvas*   $39\frac{1}{2} \times 49\frac{1}{2}$ *in.*
*Upton House, Banbury, Oxfordshire, England, National Trust*

JOHN CROME   Mousehold Heath, Norwich, about 1820   *oil on canvas*   *43¼ × 71¼ in.*
*London, Tate Gallery*

THOMAS GIRTIN  Kirkstall Abbey, about 1801  *watercolor*  *12 × 20¼ in.*
*London, Victoria and Albert Museum*

SIR THOMAS LAWRENCE   William Lock, 1790   *oil on canvas   30 × 25 in.*
*Boston, Mass., Museum of Fine Arts*

SIR THOMAS LAWRENCE  Mrs. Wolff, completed 1815  *oil on canvas  $50\frac{3}{8} \times 40\frac{1}{4}$ in.*
*Chicago,  Art Institute, Kimball Collection*

JOSEPH MALLORD WILLIAM TURNER  Buttermere Lake, with part of Cromack Water, Cumberland: a Shower, about 1798  *oil on canvas*  *35 × 47 in.*
*London, Tate Gallery*

JOSEPH MALLORD WILLIAM TURNER   The Bay of Baiae, with Apollo and the Sibyl,  about 1823
*oil on canvas   57½ × 93½ in.*
*London, Tate Gallery*

JOSEPH MALLORD WILLIAM TURNER  The Slave Ship, 1840  *oil on canvas*  $35\frac{3}{4} \times 48$ *in.*
*Boston, Mass., Museum of Fine Arts*

JOHN CONSTABLE  Stratford Mill on the Stour, 1820  *oil on canvas  50 × 72 in.*
*Cottesbrooke Hall, Northampton, England, collection Major and the Hon. Mrs. Macdonald-Buchanan*

JOHN CONSTABLE  The Leaping Horse (study), about 1825  *oil on canvas  51 × 74 in.*
*London, Victoria and Albert Museum*

JOHN CONSTABLE   Old Sarum, 1834   *watercolor*   $11\frac{7}{8} \times 19\frac{1}{4}$ *in.*
*London, Victoria and Albert Museum*

JOHN SELL COTMAN   The Ploughed Field, 1810   *watercolor   9¼ × 14 in.*
*Leeds, England, City Art Gallery*

DAVID COX  Rhyl Sands, about 1854  *oil on canvas  18 × 24½ in.*
*Manchester, England, City Art Gallery*

SIR DAVID WILKIE   The Blind Fiddler, 1806   *oil on wood   23 × 31 in.*
*London, Tate Gallery*

WILLIAM ETTY   The Storm, 1830   *oil on canvas*   $35\frac{1}{2} \times 41\frac{1}{2}$ *in.*
*Manchester, England, City Art Gallery*

RICHARD PARKES BONINGTON    Le Parterre d'Eau, Versailles, 1826    *oil on canvas    16⅝ × 20¼ in.*
*Paris, Louvre*

SIR EDWIN LANDSEER   The Challenge, 1844   *oil on canvas   38 × 83 in.*
*Lesbury House, Alnmouth, England, collection the Duke of Northumberland*

SAMUEL PALMER  Coming from Evening Church, 1830  *tempera on canvas  12 × 7¾ in.*
*London, Tate Gallery*

WILLIAM DYCE  Gethsemane, about 1860  *oil on board*  *$16\frac{1}{2} \times 12\frac{3}{8}$ in.*
*Liverpool, England, Walker Art Gallery*

GEORGE FREDERIC WATTS  The Wounded Heron, about 1837  *oil on canvas  36 × 28 in.*
*Compton, Surrey, England, Watts Gallery*

WILLIAM HOLMAN HUNT  The Scapegoat, 1856  *oil on canvas*  $33\frac{1}{2} \times 54\frac{1}{2}$ *in.*
*Port Sunlight, Cheshire, England, Lady Lever Art Gallery*

WILLIAM POWELL FRITH   The Railway Station (detail) completed 1862   *oil on canvas   45¼ × 98¼ in.*
*Egham, Surrey, England, Royal Holloway College*

FORD MADOX BROWN  Work, 1852-65  *oil on canvas*  *53 × 77½ in.*
*Manchester, England, City Art Gallery*

DANTE GABRIEL ROSSETTI  The Annunciation, 1850
*oil on canvas mounted on wood  $28\frac{1}{2} \times 16\frac{1}{4}$ in.*
*London, Tate Gallery*

SIR JOHN EVERETT MILLAIS  The Blind Girl, 1856  *oil on canvas*  $32\frac{1}{2} \times 24\frac{1}{2}$ *in.*
*Birmingham, England, City Museum and Art Gallery*

ARTHUR HUGHES  April Love, 1856  *oil on canvas*  $35 \times 19\frac{1}{4}$ in
*London, Tate Gallery*

ROBERT FEKE   Isaac Royall and his Family, 1741   *oil on canvas*   $54\frac{3}{8} \times 77\frac{3}{4}$ *in.*
*Cambridge, Mass., Harvard Law School*

JOHN SMIBERT   Bishop Berkeley and his Family, 1729   *oil on canvas*   *69½ × 93 in.*
*New Haven, Conn., Yale University Art Gallery*

JOHN SINGLETON COPLEY  Mrs. Thomas Boylston, 1765  *oil on canvas*  $50\frac{1}{2} \times 40\frac{1}{2}$ *in.*
*Cambridge, Mass., Fogg Art Museum*

JOHN SINGLETON COPLEY  Watson and the Shark, 1778   *oil on canvas   72⅛ × 90¼ in.*
*Boston, Mass., Museum of Fine Arts*

CHARLES WILLSON PEALE   The Staircase Group
1795   *oil on canvas*   89 × 39½ *in.*
*Philadelphia, Museum of Art, George W. Elkins Collection*

GILBERT STUART  Mr. Grant Skating, 1782  *oil on canvas  95¼ × 57⅛ in.*
*Washington, D. C., National Gallery of Art, Mellon Collection*

JOHN TRUMBULL  The Battle of Bunker's Hill, 1786  *oil on canvas  25 × 34 in.*
*New Haven, Conn., Yale University Art Gallery*

WASHINGTON ALLSTON  The Deluge, 1804  *oil on canvas  48 × 65¾ in.*
*New York, Metropolitan Museum of Art, Gift of William Merritt Chase,* 1909

THOMAS COLE   The Oxbow of the Connecticut, 1836   *oil on canvas   $51\frac{1}{2} \times 76$ in.*
*New York, Metropolitan Museum of Art, Gift of Mrs. Russell Sage, 1908*

WILLIAM SIDNEY MOUNT  Raffling for the Goose, 1837   *oil on wood*   17 × 23⅛ *in.*
*New York, Metropolitan Museum of Art, Gift of John D. Crimmins, 1897*

GEORGE CALEB BINGHAM  Fur Traders Descending the Missouri, about 1845  *oil on canvas  29 × 36 in.*
*New York, Metropolitan Museum of Art, Morris K. Jesup Fund, 1933*

ANTOINE SEBASTIEN PLAMONDON  Soeur St. Alphonse, 1841  *oil on canvas  36 × 28¼ in.*
*Ottawa, National Gallery of Canada*

CORNELIUS KRIEGHOFF  Merrymaking, 1860  *oil on canvas*  $34\frac{1}{4} \times 48$ *in.*
*Fredericton, New Brunswick, Canada, Beaverbrook Art Gallery*

GEORGE INNESS  Autumn Oaks, about 1875   *oil on canvas*   *21⅞ × 30¼ in.*
*New York, Metropolitan Museum of Art, Gift of George I. Seney, 1887*

# Drawings

NICHOLAS HILLIARD   Queen Elizabeth, about 1584
*pen and ink wash over pencil    diameter 5 in.*
*London, British Museum*

ISAAC OLIVER  A Lady Leaning on a Pedestal  *pen and brown ink with wash*  $3\frac{3}{4} \times 2\frac{7}{8}$ *in.*
*Oxford, Ashmolean Museum*

INIGO JONES  A Page like a Fiery Spirit, 1613
*pen and ink with watercolor  11⅜ × 7¾ in.*
*Chatsworth, England, Trustees of the Chatsworth Settlement*

INIGO JONES  Night Scene from "Luminalia," 1638  *pen and black ink with dark gray wash*  $6\frac{3}{8} \times 8\frac{3}{4}$ *in.*
*Chatsworth, England, Trustees of the Chatsworth Settlement*

SIR PETER LELY Self-portrait, 1650-55 *black chalk heightened with white* 15¼ × 12⅜ in.
*In the possession of the Lely family*

SIR GODFREY KNELLER  A Doe  *chalk*  $12\frac{1}{4} \times 10$ in.
*London, British Museum*

MARCELLUS LAROON the Younger   A Concert at Montagu House, 1735
*pencil, ink and wash   15⅜ × 11 in.*
*London, Courtauld Institute Galleries*

WILLIAM HOGARTH   The Industrious 'Prentice Performing the Duties of a Christian, about 1747    *indian ink*    $10\frac{3}{4} \times 13\frac{3}{4}$ *in.*
*London, British Museum*

ALLAN RAMSAY   Study of a Child Holding a Cat, about 1760
*black and white chalk on blue paper   $15\frac{3}{4} \times 10\frac{7}{8}$ in.*
*Edinburgh, National Gallery of Scotland*

RICHARD WILSON  Tall Trees. about 1756  *black chalk heightened with white*  $15\frac{3}{4} \times 10\frac{1}{4}$ *in.*

HN BAPTIST MALCHAIR   St. Barnabas, Oxford, 1782   *watercolor over pencil*   $10\frac{1}{2} \times 13\frac{5}{8}$ in.
*ford, Ashmolean Museum*

PAUL SANDBY  Two Ladies Seen from Behind, about 1774  *red chalk*  $7\frac{1}{4} \times 5\frac{3}{8}$ in.
*Windsor, Royal Collection*

THOMAS GAINSBOROUGH  A Lady Seated, about 1760  *black and white chalk*  $12\frac{1}{2} \times 9\frac{1}{4}$ *in.*
*Keswick, England, collection Dr. F. Springell*

THOMAS GAINSBOROUGH  A Woodland Road, about 1770  *pen, sepia and ink wash*  7 × 8¾in.
*London, British Museum*

ALEXANDER COZENS  The Cloud  *gray and black wash*  8¼ × 12 in.
*London, collection D. L. T. Oppé and Miss Oppé*

JOHN CONSTABLE  An Ash Tree, about 1835
*pencil and watercolor   39 × 26¾ in.*
*London, Victoria and Albert Museum*

CONSTABLE  Dedham, Rain Coming Up, about 1817   *pencil   4⅝ × 6¼ in.*
*no, California, Henry E. Huntington Art Gallery*

WILLIAM BLAKE  The Stoning of Achan, about 1800-5  *pen, ink and watercolor*  $15 \times 13\frac{1}{4}$ in.
*London, Tate Gallery*

GEORGE ROMNEY  The Weird Sisters, 1780
*pen, brown ink and sepia over pencil  12 × 19⅛ in.*
*Cambridge, England, Fitzwilliam Museum*

HENRY FUSELI
Perseus Returning the Eye of the Graii
*pen, ink and wash  7½ × 6¼ in.*
*Birmingham, England, City Art Gallery*

THOMAS ROWLANDSON   The Exhibition Staircase, about 1800   *pen and wash*   *15⅛ × 10¾ in.*
*Formerly London, University College, the drawing was destroyed in World War II*

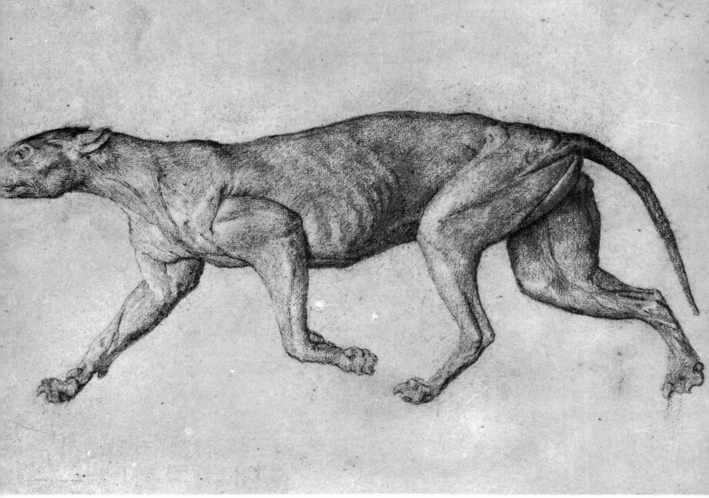

GEORGE STUBBS  A Tiger, after 1795   *ink and red chalk*   *10 × 14¼ in.*
*Worcester, Mass., Free Public Library*

SAMUEL PALMER   Self-portrait, about 1826   *black chalk heightened with white*   $11\frac{1}{4} \times 9$ *in.*
*Oxford, Ashmolean Museum*

SAMUEL PALMER  The Valley Thick with Corn, 1825  *pen and wash with sepia*  $7\frac{1}{4} \times 10\frac{7}{8}$ *in.*
*Oxford, Ashmolean Museum*

SIR DAVID WILKIE The Artist's Sister, 1833
*black and red chalk with watercolor over pencil 18¾ × 13¾ in.*
*Oxford, Ashmolean Museum*

SIR THOMAS LAWRENCE Mrs. Linley
about 1790 *pencil 9 × 7¼ in.*
*Upperville, Virginia, collection Mr. Paul Mellon*

ALFRED STEVENS  A Young Girl
about 1859  *pencil heightened with crayon and gouache*  15⅛ × 10⅛ in.
*Oxford, Ashmolean Museum*

RICHARD PARKES BONINGTON  St. Wulfran, Abbeville, 1818
*pencil heightened with white*  $9\frac{3}{8} \times 7\frac{1}{8}$ in.
*Paris, Louvre*

JAMES HOLLAND   The Tower of St. Lawrence, Rotterdam, about 1845   *pencil and watercolor heightened with white*   $11\frac{3}{4} \times 17\frac{1}{8}$ in.
*Manchester, England, Whitworth Art Gallery*

JOSEPH MALLORD WILLIAM TURNER  Tivoli  *watercolor  11¾ × 17 in.*
*Manchester, England, Whitworth Art Gallery*

JOSEPH MALLORD WILLIAM TURNER  Venice, Calm at Sunrise, about 1843
*watercolor  8¾ × 12½ in.*
*Cambridge, England, Fitzwilliam Museum*

JOHN RUSKIN  Coast Scene near Dunbar, 1857  *pen and watercolor  12¼ × 18¼ in.*
*Birmingham, England, City Art Gallery*

EDWARD LEAR  Cliffs at Grammatico, Paxos, 1863
*watercolor  12⅝ × 9¼ in.*
*San Marino, California, Henry E. Huntington Art Gallery*

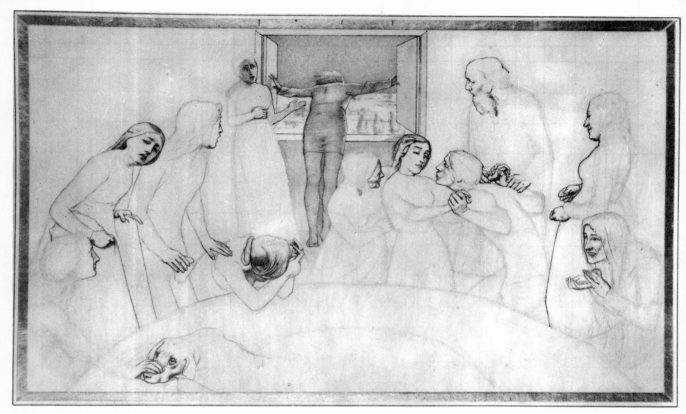

SIR JOHN EVERETT MILLAIS  The Deluge, 1849/50  *pencil finished with ink*  $9\frac{1}{2} \times 16\frac{3}{4}$ *in.*
*London, British Museum*

DANTE GABRIEL ROSSETTI  Miss Siddal, 1855  *pen and brown and black ink*  $4\frac{3}{4} \times 4\frac{1}{4}$ *in.*
*Oxford, Ashmolean Museum*

JOHN SINGLETON COPLEY  Earl Bathurst, about 1781  *black chalk heightened with white*  *26 × 19 in.*
*Boston, Museum of Fine Arts*

WASHINGTON ALLSTON   A Ship at Sea   *chalk on canvas*   47½ × 59½ *in.*
*ridge, Mass., Fogg Art Museum, Harvard University.   On loan Washington Allston Trust*

**WILLIAM SIDNEY MOUNT**  Portrait of a Lady, 1842   *pencil on white paper*   $9\frac{3}{4} \times 7\frac{5}{8}$ *in.*
*Cambridge, Mass., Fogg Art Museum, Harvard University*

# Sculpture

PIETRO TORRIGIANO   The Tomb of Henry VII and Margaret of York
1509-17   *bronze*
*London, Westminster Abbey*

MAXIMILIAN COLT Monument to the Countess of Derby  *marble*

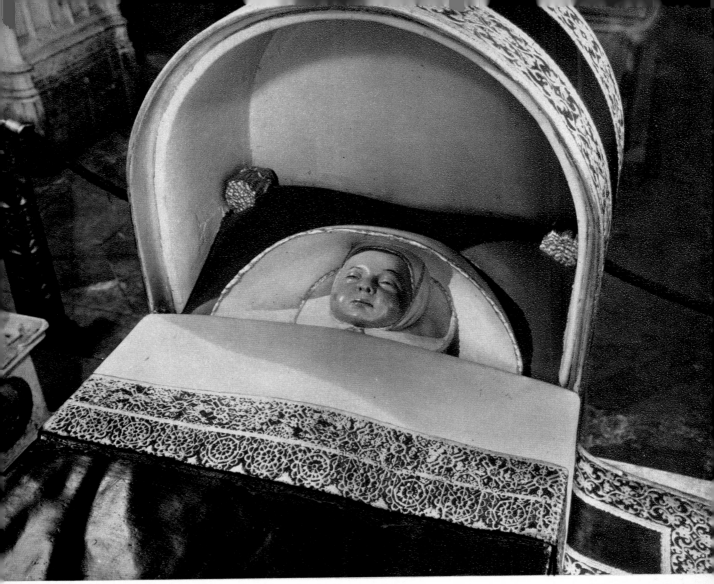

MAXIMILIAN COLT · The Tomb of Princess Sophia, about 1607 *stone* *52×51 in.*
*h, Westminster Abbey*

OHN BUSHNELL  Charles I, 1671  *stone*
*ondon, Old Bailey*

HUBERT LE SUEUR   Equestrian Statue of Charles I, 1633   *bronze*
*London, Charing Cross*

NICHOLAS STONE
Monument to John Donne
about 1631   *marble*
*London, St. Paul's Cathedral*

CAIUS GABRIEL CIBBER   Monument to the Sackville Family, 1677   *marble*
*Withyham, England, Parish Church*

GRINLING GIBBONS  James II, 1686  *bronze*
*London, Trafalgar Square*

JOHN VAN NOST   Monument to the 3rd Earl of Bristol, 1608   *marble*

LOUIS FRANÇOIS ROUBILIAC  Monument to Lady Elizabeth Nightingale, 1761  *marble*
*London, Westminster Abbey*

EDWARD PIERCE  Sir Christopher Wren, about 1673  *marble*
*Oxford, Ashmolean Museum*

JOHN MICHAEL RYSBRACK  Alexander Pope, 1730
*marble  height 27 in.*
*London, Athenaeum Club*

**JOHN BACON** Dr. Johnson, about 1770 *marble height 30 in.*
*Oxford, Pembroke College*

ER SCHEEMAKERS Sir Justinian Isham, about 1737 *marble height 24 in.*
*mpton, England, collection Sir Gyles Isham*

CHRISTOPHER HEWETSON   The Duke of Gloucester, 1772
*arble   height 23 in.*
*Vindsor, Royal Collection*

JOSEPH NOLLEKENS   William Weddell, 1789   *marble heigh*
*Ripon, England, collection Major Edward Compton*

FLAXMAN  Monument to Dr. Warton, 1801

*ester, England, Cathedral*

JOSEPH WILTON  Monument to General Wolfe, 1772  *marble*
*London, Westminster Abbey*

THOMAS BANKS  Monument to Captain Burgess, 1802  *marble*
*London, St. Paul's Cathedral*

SACRED TO THE MEMORY OF
ELLEN JANE AND MARIANNE,
ONLY CHILDREN
OF THE LATE REV? WILLIAM ROBINSON,
AND ELLEN JANE HIS WIFE
THEIR AFFECTIONATE MOTHER,
IN FOND REMEMBRANCE OF THEIR "HEAV'N LOV'D INNOCENCE,"
CONSIGNS THEIR RESEMBLANCES TO THIS SANCTUARY,
IN HUMBLE GRATITUDE
FOR THE GLORIOUS ASSURANCE, THAT
"OF SUCH IS THE KINGDOM OF GOD"

FRANCIS CHANTREY   Monument to the Children of the Rev. W. Robinson, 1812   *marble*
*d, England, Cathedral*

JOHN GIBSON  Narcissus, 1829  *marble*
*London, Royal Academy*

WILLIAM RUSH  George Washington, 1814  *marble*
*Philadelphia, Independence Hall*

THOMAS WOOLNER
Lord Tennyson, 1857  *marble*
*Cambridge, England, Trinity College*

HIRAM POWERS  The Greek Slave, 1846
*marble   height 65 in.*
*Washington, D. C., Corcoran Art Gallery*

# Influences and
# Developments

Hans Holbein the Younger
Henry Howard, Earl of Surrey *chalk, pen and wash* $9\frac{7}{8} \times 8\frac{1}{8}$ *in.*
*Windsor, Royal Collection*

a

b

**a** Miguel Sithium
Henry VII, 1505
*oil on panel   14½ × 9¼ in.*
*London, National Portrait Gallery*

**b** Hans Holbein the Younger
Henry VIII (detail)
*oil on oak   10¾ × 7¾ in.*
*Lugano, Thyssen Collection*

**c** Hans Holbein the Younger
Sir Thomas More, 1527
*oil on wood   29½ × 24 in.*
*New York, Frick Collection*

**d** Hans Holbein the Younger
Sir Thomas More
(detail of **c**)

**e** Hans Holbein the Younger
The Duchess of Milan, 1538
*oil on oak   70¼ × 32¼ in.*
*London, National Gallery*

**f** Hans Holbein the Younger
The Duchess of Milan
(detail of **e**)

**g** Anonymous
Margaret, Countess of Salisbury
*oil on panel   24 × 19 in.*
*London, National Portrait Gallery*

**h** John Bettes
Man in a Black Cap, 1545
*oil on oak   18½ × 16⅛ in.*
*London, Tate Gallery*

**i** Anonymous
Queen Elizabeth I, about 1575
*oil on panel   31 × 24 in.*
*Liverpool, England, Walker Art Gallery*

c

d

## The Beginnings of English Portraiture

Hans Holbein the Younger, who became Court Painter to Henry VIII in the 1530's, was a superb draftsman. His portraits were usually painted from clear, linear preliminary drawings, a number of which are in the Royal Library at Windsor Castle. One of his masterpieces is the portrait of the young widowed Duchess of Milan (e, f) painted at Brussels in 1538, when Henry had her in mind as a prospective bride. Happily for her she married the Duke of Lorraine. The majority of English 16th-century portraits are by unknown artists, although scholars are now beginning to identify some of them. Most, like John Bettes, worked in a style very close to that of Holbein.

e

f

g

h

i

## 17th-Century Portraiture: its Sources and Foreign Influences

Anthony van Dyck first came to London from Antwerp in 1620 and was for a short time attached to the court of James I. He spent the years 1621-27 in Italy. In 1632 he returned to England, became Court Painter to Charles I and brought to English painting a sophisticated and European elegance. The portraits of other painters established in England, such as Daniel Mytens (a), a Dutchman, and Cornelius Johnson (c), of Flemish extraction, appear somewhat gauche when set beside his.

Van Dyck painted a number of portraits of the king and queen and their children. The three heads of Charles on one canvas (e) and the profile of Henrietta

a

b

c

d

e

f

212

Maria (f) were painted to be sent to Rome so that Bernini might make marble busts from them. The bust of Charles was completed, but perished in the fire at Whitehall Palace in 1688. The great portrait of Charles I on horseback (i) was inspired by Titian's portrait of the Emperor Charles V at the Battle of Mühlberg (h).

g

h

i

**a** Daniel Mytens
Charles I, 1623
*oil on canvas 80⅜ × 51 in.*
*Windsor, Royal Collection*

**b** Sir Anthony van Dyck
Charles I, 1636
*oil on canvas 97¾ × 60½ in.*
*Windsor, Royal Collection*

**c** Cornelius Johnson
Unknown Lady, 1630
*oil on canvas 79 × 49 in.*
*Drumlanrig Castle, Scotland,*
*collection the Duke of*
*Buccleuch and Queensberry*

**d** Sir Anthony van Dyck
Martha, Countess of Monmouth
*oil on canvas 85½ × 50 in.*
*Longford Castle, Wiltshire, England*
*collection the Earl of Radnor*

**e** Sir Anthony van Dyck
Charles I. Three Heads on One
Canvas, about 1636
*oil on canvas 33¼ × 39¼ in.*
*Windsor, Royal Collection*

**f** Sir Anthony van Dyck
Henrietta Maria
*oil on canvas 28¼ × 22¼ in.*
*Windsor, Royal Collection*

**g** Sir Anthony van Dyck
Sir Thomas Hanmer
*oil on canvas 42 × 34 in.*
*Weston Park, Shropshire, England,*
*collection the Earl of Bradford*

**h** Titian
Charles V on Horseback, 1548
*oil on canvas 126¾ × 109⅞ in.*
*Madrid, Prado*

**i** Sir Anthony van Dyck
Charles I on Horseback
*oil on canvas 144 × 114 in.*
*London, National Gallery*

## Charles I as an Art Collector

Charles I was perhaps the most gifted collector of works of art that Europe has ever known, but it should not be forgotten that Thomas Howard, Earl of Arundel, (1586-1646) set him the example. Arundel was celebrated for his collection of antique sculpture. In the portrait of him by Mytens, or Van Somer, (a) he is shown sitting at the entrance to the sculpture gallery in his house in the Strand, London.

In 1627 Charles bought the greater part of the collection of paintings formed by the Dukes of Mantua. This included the Mantegna cartoons, *The Triumphs of Caesar*, now at Hampton Court (i). A few years earlier in 1623 he had purchased in Genoa Raphael's magnificent cartoons for the Vatican tapestries (j). Rembrandt's portrait of *The Artist's Mother* (h) was in his collection before 1639.

Other well-known items from his collection are shown here. Raphael's little *St. George and the Dragon* (f) was perhaps the first important Italian picture ever to come to England. It was painted for Federico da Montefeltro, Duke of Urbino, and was sent by him as a gift to Henry VII. Charles I's collection was largely dispersed by sale on the orders of the Commonwealth government.

a

c

d

b

e

214

f

g

h

i

j

**a** Daniel Mytens
Thomas Howard, Earl of Arundel,
about 1620
*oil on canvas   80 × 50 in.*
*Arundel, Sussex, England,*
*collection the Duke of Norfolk*

**b** Sir Anthony van Dyck
Cupid and Psyche
*oil on canvas   78½ × 75½ in.*
*Buckingham Palace, Royal Collection*

**c** Titian
The Entombment
*oil on canvas   58¾ × 84¾ in.*
*Paris, Louvre*

**d** Arundel Marble — The Tomb
of Phylista
*marble   70 × 32 in.*
*Oxford, Ashmolean Museum*

**e** Titian
The Pardo Venus
*oil on canvas   77½ × 151½ in.*
*Paris, Louvre*

**f** Raphael
St. George and the Dragon,
about 1505
*oil on panel   11⅛ × 8½ in.*
*Washington, National Gallery,*
*Mellon Collection*

**g** Giorgione
Fête Champêtre
*oil on canvas   43½ × 54¼ in.*
*Paris, Louvre*

**h** Rembrandt
The Artist's Mother, about 1630
*oil on panel   23½ × 18 in.*
*Buckingham Palace, Royal Collection*

**i** Mantegna
The Triumphs of Caesar —
The Elephants (detail), 1494
*tempera on canvas   108⅝ × 108⅝ in.*
*Hampton Court, Royal Collection*

**j** Raphael
Paul and Barnabus at Lystra,
about 1516
*tempera on paper 136½ × 213¼ in.*
*London, Victoria and Albert Museum,*
*Royal Collection*

215

Peter Lely arrived in England from Haarlem in about 1643 and soon took over much of the practice established by van Dyck, who had died in 1641. During the Civil War he received commissions from sitters belonging to both political parties; after the Restoration he became Court Painter to Charles II. Two series of portraits show his abilities at their best, the Admirals now in the National Maritime Museum at Greenwich, London, and the "Beauties" at Hampton Court.

a

b

c

**a** Sir Peter Lely
Portrait of a Sculptor, about 1646
*oil on canvas* $40 \times 32\frac{1}{2}$ *in.*
*Chatsworth, Trustees of the*
*Chatsworth Settlement*

**b** Sir Peter Lely
Oliver Cromwell, about 1653
*oil on canvas* $30 \times 24\frac{3}{4}$ *in.*
*Birmingham, England,*
*City Museum and Art Gallery*

**c** Robert Walker
Oliver Cromwell
*oil on canvas* $49\frac{1}{2} \times 39\frac{1}{2}$ *in.*
*London, National Portrait Gallery*

**d** Sir Peter Lely
Lady Byron as St. Catharine
*oil on canvas* $62\frac{3}{4} \times 52\frac{1}{4}$ *in.*
*Hampton Court, Royal Collection*

**e** Sir Peter Lely
Barbara, Duchess of Cleveland
*oil on canvas* $74 \times 50\frac{1}{2}$ *in.*
*Knole, collection Lord Sackville*

d

e

Lely died in 1680. Godfrey Kneller, a painter of German origin who had settled in London in 1674, succeeded him as the leading portrait painter of the country just as Lely had succeeded van Dyck. Like Lely he was a painter of unequal merit, but at its best his style was bold and masculine.

Both Lely and Kneller dominated their generation and to some extent inhibited the development of a native English school of painting. But there were some artists of distinct individuality working at this time—William Dobson, Robert Walker, and John Riley chief among them.

f

g

h

i

j

k

**f** Sir Godfrey Kneller
The Duchess of Marlborough
*oil on canvas   65 × 61 in.*
*Petworth House, Sussex, England,*
*Petworth Collection*

**g** Sir Godfrey Kneller
William Congreve, 1709
*oil on canvas   36 × 28 in.*
*London, National Portrait Gallery*

**h** Jonathan Richardson
Edward Colston, about 1710
*oil on canvas   49 × 40 in.*
*Bristol, England, The Council House*

**i** John Riley
Bridget Holmes, 1686
*oil on canvas   88¾ × 58¼ in.*
*St. James's Palace, Royal Collection*

**j** Sir Godfrey Kneller
Jacob Tonson, 1717
*oil on canvas   36 × 28 in.*
*London, National Portrait Gallery*

**k** Charles Jervas
Dean Swift
*oil on canvas   48½ × 38¼ in.*
*London, National Portrait Gallery*

a

d

e

William Hogarth is frequently cited as the first outstanding English painter. This is not strictly true, but certainly there had been no one before him with such an active variety of gifts or with so pugnacious an English temperament. Hogarth's

b

c

f

most original contribution to English painting was in the field of illustration. He invented his own lively form of the moral narrative picture, but his portraits are of almost equal importance (b, e, i). In them he set out to show that an Englishman could paint as ably and attractively as foreigners like van Loo, the Frenchman (a), or the Venetian Amigoni (d), who had a fashionable following in London. His *Captain Coram*, painted as a gift to the Foundling Hospital, and partly based on the engraving of Rigaud's *Samuel Bernard* (c), is the first English portrait to master the Baroque idiom.

English painting grew progressively livelier. Painters like Hayman and Highmore had a French lightness of touch (f, g). But it was Allan Ramsay (h, j), a Scottish painter who had studied in Italy, who assimilated continental elegance with the greatest ease. The difference between his early portraits and his later ones is most marked.

g

h

i

j

## The Rise of the Grand Manner

a

As the 18th century progressed, more and more young Englishmen of the titled and upper classes made the Grand Tour of Europe. They amassed collections of old masters and sculpture and views of the places they had visited, and these formed the basis of the great English country house collections.

Sir Joshua Reynolds, first President of the Royal Academy, extolled the Grand Manner in painting; that is, the style which looks to antique sculpture and to Italian High Renaissance painting for its models. The *Apollo Belvedere* in the Vatican Gallery was especially admired (g), and suggested the pose for a number of full length male portraits of the time. Subjects from classical history or mythology were attempted by all serious artists, but not always with success.

b

c

d

e

a  Batoni
Douglas, 8th Duke of Hamilton
1775
*oil on canvas   89 × 65 in.*
*Inveraray Castle, Scotland,*
*collection the Duke of Argyll*

b  Vanvitelli
The Colosseum
*oil on canvas   32½ × 51 in.*
*Holkham, Norfolk, England,*
*collection the Earl of Leicester*

c  Gavin Hamilton
Dr. J. Moore, the 8th Duke of
Hamilton, and Ensign Moore
*oil on canvas   83 × 60 in.*
*Haddington, East Lothian, Scotland,*
*collection the Duke of Hamilton*

d  Canaletto
View of the Bacino di San Marco,
1725-30
*oil on canvas   55½ × 60 in.*
*Cardiff, National Museum of Wales*

e  Johann Zoffany
Charles Towneley with his Marbles
*oil on canvas   50 × 40 in.*
*Burnley, England, Towneley Hall*
*Art Gallery and Museum*

**f**

**g**

**h**

**i**

**j**

**k**

**l**

a

## American Painters in 18th-Century London

North American painters first made their way to Europe in the middle of the 18th century. Benjamin West spent the years 1760-63 in Italy, and after that set up practice in London. He succeeded Reynolds as President of the Royal Academy in 1792. West's history pictures in the classical manner are often undistinguished, but in *The Death of Wolfe* (p. 114) he was a pioneer of history painting as a record of the contemporary scene. His pleasing portrait of his wife and child (a) is a direct reminiscence of Raphael (b).

John Singleton Copley came from Boston. Apart from lively portraits he produced large-scale history paintings of great competence which had a popular sale as engravings. Other Americans who worked for a time in England were Gilbert Stuart, Mather Brown, and John Trumbull. The young Thomas Lawrence (i) sat for Trumbull for the head of Captain José Barboza, the figure who lies dying in the center of *The Sortie from Gibraltar* (h).

b

c

d

e

f

g

h

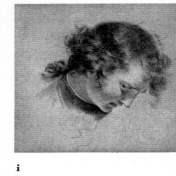

i

j

**a** Benjamin West
Mrs. West and her Son Raphael,
about 1770
*oil on canvas   $26\frac{1}{4} \times 26$ in.*
*Cleveland, Ohio, Museum of Art,*
*Charles W. Harkness Gift*

**b** Raphael
The Madonna of the Chair,
about 1514
*oil on panel   diameter 28 in.*
*Florence, Pitti Palace*

**c** Benjamin West
Queen Charlotte, 1779
*oil on canvas   $99\frac{1}{2} \times 70$ in.*
*Buckingham Palace, Royal Collection*

**d** John Singleton Copley
Mr. and Mrs. Ralph Izard, 1775
*oil on canvas   $69 \times 88$ in.*
*Boston, Mass., Museum of Fine Arts*

**e** John Singleton Copley
The Three Princesses, 1785
*oil on canvas   $104 \times 61$ in.*
*Buckingham Palace, Royal Collection*

**f** Gilbert Stuart
Sir John Hort, 1785
*oil on canvas   $30 \times 25$ in.*
*Saltram, Plymouth, England,*
*National Trust*

**g** Mather Brown
John Howard
*oil on canvas   $27 \times 23$ in.*
*London, National Portrait Gallery*

**h** John Trumbull
The Sortie from Gibraltar, 1788
*oil on canvas   $20 \times 30$ in.*
*Cincinnati, Ohio, Art Museum*

**i** John Trumbull
The Head of Thomas Lawrence,
1789
*crayon on blue paper   $14 \times 11\frac{1}{4}$ in.*
*Boston, Mass., Athenaeum*

**j** John Singleton Copley
The Death of Major Peirson, 1783
*oil on canvas   $97 \times 143$ in.*
*London, Tate Gallery*

# The Beginnings of Landscape Painting in England

Landscape painting in England developed in two distinct ways: one, the classical, based on the compositions of Claude, or in a more romantic mood on those of Salvator Rosa, and the other, more naturalistic, derived from 17th-century Dutch painters like Wynants and Ruisdael. It was, however, Richard Wilson (a) who, having spent some years in Italy in the 1750's, interpreted the Claudian landscape composition (b) to the English public. He would also sometimes paint romantic subjects (c) in the manner of Salvator (d). Wilson could create light and space in his landscapes as no painter in England had done before him, and on his return from Italy he applied this capacity to the English and Welsh landscape.

Gainsborough, who painted landscape (e) for the sheer love of it—he made his living from portraits—began in the Dutch manner (f), but when he moved from Ipswich to Bath and studied the landscape backgrounds of portraits by van Dyck that he saw in local collections, his whole concept of the painting of field and hill and foliage changed and became more free and rhythmical. In London, when he had no time for visiting the country, he would often paint imaginary landscapes based on arrangements of twig and glass and pebble which he would set out on a table in his studio—as in his *Mountain Valley with Sheep* (h).

a

b

**a** Richard Wilson
Lake Albano and Castel Gandolfo
*oil on canvas   29 × 38 in.*
*Port Sunlight, Cheshire, England,*
*Lady Lever Art Gallery*

**b** Claude
Classical Landscape, 1645
*oil on canvas   40 × 52¼ in.*
*Birmingham, England,*
*The Barber Institute of Fine Arts*

**c** Richard Wilson
The Unransomed
*oil on canvas   39 × 50 in.*
*Port Sunlight, Cheshire, England,*
*Lady Lever Art Gallery*

**d** Salvator Rosa
Rocky Landscape
*oil on canvas   39 × 43 in.*
*Holkham, Norfolk, England,*
*collection the Earl of Leicester*

c

d

e

f

e Thomas Gainsborough
Cornard Wood, about 1748
*oil on canvas   48 × 61 in.*
*London, National Gallery*

f Jan Wynants
Landscape with Dead Tree, 1659
*oil on canvas   31 × 39 in.*
*London, National Gallery*

g Thomas Gainsborough
Mary, Duchess of Richmond,
after 1774
*oil on canvas   91 × 59 in.*
*Ascott, Buckinghamshire, England,*
*National Trust*

h Thomas Gainsborough
Mountain Valley with Sheep, 1783
*oil on canvas   46 × 56 in.*
*Edinburgh, National Gallery of Scotland*

g

h

a

b

c

d

e

f

# Watercolor Painting

Watercolor painting developed rapidly in 18th-century England. The subject matter was largely topographical, and for the most part watercolor views were designed to be engraved and published in book form. At the beginning taste inclined to views which had an antiquarian interest, but gradually this gave way to the romantically picturesque. As time went on, abbeys, castles, and ruins were selected more for their scenic possibilities than for their historical associations.

Sometimes a watercolor artist would accompany a young man making the Grand Tour. The most important of these was John Robert Cozens, who went to Italy with William Beckford in 1782 (p. 116). Soon almost every artist of note who practiced in watercolor felt that it was essential to spend time traveling and working abroad.

The English watercolor school was rightly esteemed above any other. It found in Girtin and Cotman, de Wint and Cox, artists who brought to watercolor painting all the breadth of composition and freedom of technique which is possible with oils.

g

**a** Wenceslaus Hollar
A View of the Thames below Westminster Pier
*pen and ink  5¾ × 15¾ in.*
*Birmingham, England,*
*The Barber Institute of Fine Arts*

**b** Francis Place   The Dropping Well at Knaresborough
*indian ink and wash  13 × 16 in.*
*London, British Museum*

**c** John Warwick Smith   Terracina
*watercolor  7 × 10 in.*
*London, Victoria and Albert Museum*

**d** Joseph Farington
Worcester Cathedral, 1789
*watercolor  9 × 13 in.*
*London, Victoria and Albert Museum*

**e** Thomas Malton
Westminster Abbey
*watercolor  12¾ × 18⅞ in.*
*Birmingham, England, City Museum and Art Gallery*

**f** Thomas Shotter Boys
Paris, View near the Pont Royal
1829
*watercolor  13⅜ × 10⅜ in.*
*London, Victoria and Albert Museum*

**g** Samuel Prout
Porch of Ratisbon Cathedral
*watercolor  25¾ × 18¼ in.*
*London, Victoria and Albert Museum*

**h** Peter de Wint
Gloucester Cathedral
*watercolor  11⅛ × 18¼ in.*
*Bedford, England, Cecil Higgins Art Gallery*

**i** David Cox
The Night Train, about 1849
*watercolor  11 × 15 in.*
*Birmingham, England, City Museum and Art Gallery*

h

i

a

b

c

d

e

f

g

# A Change of Mood in British Painting

The end of the 18th century, which was anticipated by the French Revolution, was marked by a total change of mood—from the classical to the romantic. In portraiture this was characterized by a more theatrical and emotional presentation of the sitter, and of all the new painters the young Thomas Lawrence was the romantic portrait painter par excellence. *Elizabeth Farren* (b), which he exhibited at the Royal Academy when he was only 20 years old, is a tour de force of sparkling paint and lively charm. William Owen, Lawrence's exact contemporary, was a minor master of the romantic portrait (c) and is less known than he deserves to be.

Lawrence was a devoted student of the past, but he turned to the masters of fluent brushwork and rich spontaneous color—Rubens and Velázquez—rather than to the painters of the Italian High Renaissance who had inspired Reynolds. Of his many pupils and assistants the most distinguished was William Etty, who brought some of the vitality of Rubens to the painting of mythological and historical subjects and was one of the outstanding English colorists of his time (i).

h

**a** John Hoppner
Frances, 4th Countess of Jersey
*oil on canvas 30 × 25 in.*
*Radier Manor, Jersey, Channel Islands,*
*collection the Earl of Jersey*

**b** Sir Thomas Lawrence
Elizabeth Farren, 1790
*oil on canvas 94 × 57½ in.*
*New York, Metropolitan Museum*

**c** William Owen
Lady Leicester, 1811
*oil on canvas 92 × 55 in.*
*Tabley House, Knutsford, England,*
*collection Lt. Col. J. L. B.*
*Leicester-Warren*

**d** John Opie
Thomas Girtin
*oil on canvas 29 × 24 in.*
*London, National Portrait Gallery*

**e** Diego Velázquez
The Infanta Margarita
about 1653
*oil on canvas 40 × 39 in.*
*Vienna, Kunsthistorisches Museum*

**f** Sir Thomas Lawrence
Lady Robert Manners, 1826
*oil on canvas 54 × 43 in.*
*Edinburgh, National Gallery of Scotland*

**g** Peter Paul Rubens
A Scholar, about 1618
*oil on canvas 47 × 41 in.*
*Munich, Alte Pinakothek*

**h** Peter Paul Rubens
The Landing of Marie de Medici
at Marseilles, about 1625
*oil on canvas 155 × 116 in.*
*Paris, Louvre*

**i** William Etty
Cleopatra's Arrival in Cilicia, 1821
*oil on canvas 42 × 52 in.*
*Port Sunlight, Cheshire, England,*
*Lady Lever Art Gallery*

i

a

## William Blake and the English Romantic Movement

One usually associates the Romantic Movement with literature and especially poetry, and it is perhaps best symbolized by one man, William Blake, who was poet, painter and mystic. Blake carried even into old age the lyrical freshness and idealism of romantic youth. His faith survived periods of disillusion. The visionary quality of his work is clearly seen if one compares *Pity* (d), an interpretation of lines from *Macbeth*, with other contemporary illustrations to Shakespeare (b, e).

A revival of interest in Shakespeare had started in the middle of the 18th century. It was given an impetus in the arts by Alderman Boydell of London who, in the 1780's, commissioned a number of artists to paint scenes from Shakespeare which were then engraved and sold in book form.

Blake was not the only visionary among the Romantic painters. Fuseli, the Swiss artist who settled in London, sometimes achieved a Blake-like quality, but it was a few young men of the next generation, notably Samuel Palmer and Edward Calvert who knew Blake in old age, who, if only for a few years in the 1820's and 30's, carried his innocent clarity and inspiration into an increasingly industrial and mechanical age.

b

d

c

**a** Francis Wheatley
The Rescue of Emilia
*oil on canvas   30 × 21 in.*
*Stratford-upon-Avon, England,*
*collection of the Royal*
*Shakespeare Theater*

**b** James Northcote
The Murder of the Princes in
the Tower, 1786
*oil on canvas   70 × 54 in.*
*Petworth House, England,*
*Petworth Collection*

**c** Robert Smirke
Falstaff at Herne's Oak, about 1793
*oil on canvas   30 × 21 in.*
*Stratford-upon-Avon, England,*
*collection of the Royal*
*Shakespeare Theater*

**d** William Blake
Pity, about 1795
*color print   16 × 21 in.*
*London, Tate Gallery*

**e** George Romney
Shakespeare Attended by Nature
and the Passions
*oil on canvas   18 × 24 in.*
*Stratford-upon-Avon, England,*
*collection of the Royal Shakespeare*
*Theater*

e

f

g

h

i

j

k

**f** William Blake
Glad Day
*color print   $11 \times 7$ in.*
*London, British Museum*

**g** William Blake
Illustration to Thornton's
"Virgil," 1821
*wood engraving*
*London, British Museum*

**h** Henry Fuseli
Solitude: Morning Twilight
about 1795
*oil on canvas   $43\frac{1}{8} \times 32\frac{1}{4}$ in.*
*Zürich, collection Dr. Konrad Ulrich*

**i** Samuel Palmer
Sleeping Shepherd, about 1833
*tempera   $15 \times 20\frac{1}{4}$ in.*
*Pitswood, Horsham, Sussex, England,*
*collection Mr. J. G. Pilcher*

**j** George Richmond
The Eve of Separation, 1830
*watercolor and copal varnish on panel*
*$19 \times 14$ in.*
*Oxford, Ashmolean Museum*

**k** Edward Calvert
Pastoral Landscape
*oil on paper   $14\frac{3}{8} \times 10\frac{5}{8}$ in.*
*Oxford, Ashmolean Museum*

**a** John Constable
The Hay-Wain, 1821
*oil on canvas   51 × 73 in.*
*London, National Gallery*

**b** John Constable
The Hay-Wain (detail of **a**)

**c** John Constable
Salisbury Cathedral from the
Water-Meadows, 1831
*oil on canvas   60 × 75 in.*
*Broadwell Hill, Moreton-in-Marsh,*
*England, collection Lord Ashton of Hyde*

**d** Jacob van Ruisdael
The Jewish Cemetery, about 1660
*oil on canvas   56 × 74 in.*
*Detroit, Institute of Arts*

**e** Joseph Mallord William Turner
Dido Building Carthage, 1815
*oil on canvas   61 × 91 in.*
*London, National Gallery*

**f** Claude
Embarkation of the Queen of Sheba
1648
*oil on canvas   58 × 76 in.*
*London, National Gallery*

**g** Joseph Mallord William Turner
Rain, Steam and Speed, 1844
*oil on canvas   35 × 48 in.*
*London, National Gallery*

**h** Claude Monet
Houses of Parliament: Sun coming
through Fog, 1904
*oil on canvas   32 × 36 in.*
*Paris, Louvre*

## The Great 19th-Century Landscape Painters

Constable and Turner who, without being conscious of it, effected a revolution in English painting, were both artists with a reverence for the masters of the past. Constable, for instance, based the composition of his splendidly romantic *Salisbury Cathedral from the Water-Meadows* (c) on Ruisdael's *Jewish Cemetery* (d). His development as an artist, however, owed less to his study of other paintings than to the keenness of his observation of the countryside and his countryman's familiarity with country ways. No one before him had been so free from inhibitions as to how, or in what color key, the English landscape should be painted.

Turner spent much time traveling in Europe, whereas Constable never went abroad. He occasionally vied with old masters such as Claude (f), but he was progressively more and more obsessed by painting as an exercise in color for its own sake. Forms dissolve in mists, and records of Venice or the Rhineland melt into color-visions. In a late work like *Rain, Steam and Speed* (g), which shows a locomotive speeding over the railway bridge at Maidenhead, he anticipated the painting of the French Impressionists (h).

**a**

**b**

c

d

e

f

g

h

**a**

## Romantic Painting

The Romantic Movement was European in origin and extent and its finest expression was achieved in France. Géricault and Delacroix were its greatest exponents.

The Romantics were concerned not only with new freedom in the techniques of painting but also with new kinds of subject matter. The powerful, the heroic, the tragic occupied their thoughts and ambitions. These were emotions in which English artists had not generally indulged, but the new generation, men like James Ward in particular, were wholly in sympathy with the atmosphere of romanticism.

Another aspect of the romantic imagination was a looking back to the past. Narrative subjects were sought in history—especially medieval history—and in literature. There was, too, a glorification of great men, heroes, kings and poets.

America was well aware of the Romantic Movement, and Washington Allston and Thomas Cole were as romantic in their choice of subject as any European.

**b**

**c**

**d**

**e**

**f**

g

h

i

j

k

l

**a** John Martin
Sadak in Search of the Waters
of Oblivion, about 1815
*oil on canvas   30 × 28 in.*
*Southampton, England, Art Gallery*

**b** James Ward
Gordale Scar, Yorkshire, about 1815
*oil on canvas   131 × 166 in.*
*London, Tate Gallery*

**c** James Ward
Napoleon's Horse Marengo, 1824
*oil on canvas   32 × 43 in.*
*Alnwick, collection the Duke*
*of Northumberland*

**d** Theodore Géricault
Frightened Horse, about 1813
*oil on canvas   19 × 24 in.*
*London, National Gallery*

**e** Thomas Cole
Abel, 1832
*oil on wooden panel   17½ × 29 in.*
*New York, Albany Institute*

**f** Theodore Géricault
The Raft of the Medusa, 1818
*oil on canvas   193 × 282 in.*
*Paris, Louvre*

**g** Richard Parkes Bonington
Francis I and Margaret
of Navarre, 1827
*oil on canvas   18 × 13½ in.*
*London, Wallace Collection*

**h** Eugène Delacroix
Hamlet and Horatio in
the Cemetery
*oil on canvas   32 × 25 in.*
*Paris, Louvre*

**i** Benjamin Haydon
Wordsworth, 1842
*oil on canvas   49 × 39 in.*
*London, National Portrait Gallery*

**j** Sir David Wilkie
The Entrance of George IV into
Holyrood, 1830
*oil on canvas   69 × 95 in.*
*Holyrood, Scotland, Royal Collection*

**k** Charles Eastlake
The Champion, 1824
*oil on canvas   48 × 69 in.*
*Birmingham, England,*
*City Museum and Art Gallery*

**l** Washington Allston
The Flight of Florimell, 1819
*oil on canvas   36 × 28 in.*
*Detroit, Institute of Art*

**a**

**b**

## American Painting (17th-19th centuries)

Painting properly began in America during the 17th century with the artist-explorers and a number of anonymous artists such as the "Freake Limner" (a), who painted portraits in a naïve provincial style based on the Dutch and English traditions.

In the first half of the 18th century the European trend is strongly reflected in portraits by John Smibert (b) (and p. 148), Robert Feke (p. 147), and others. Perhaps the greatest artist of 18th-century America was John Singleton Copley (pp. 149-50). Towards the end of the century native-born artists like Benjamin West (p. 114), and Gilbert Stuart (p. 152) received their training in Europe and subsequently had a considerable influence on the development of American art, especially on the work of Charles Willson Peale (p. 151), and the history-painter John Trumbull (p. 153). By 1800, however, a distinct American School was evident in portraiture, landscape, still-life, and genre-painting characterized by the choice of American subject matter and the blending of native genius with influences from abroad.

The impact of the Romantic movement in Europe reached America in the early years of the 19th century, mainly by way of the landscapes and genre-scenes of Washington Allston (p. 154), who tempered his poetical and lyrical representations with a certain down-to-earth realism. Landscape remained popular throughout the century, flourishing especially in the work of the Hudson River School from about 1825 to about 1870. Under the leadership of Thomas Cole (p. 155) a number of painters including Asher Brown Durand, John Frederick Kensett, and

**a** 'The Freake Limner'
Mrs. Elizabeth Freake and
Baby Mary, about 1674
*oil on canvas  42¼ × 36¾ in.*
*Worcester, Mass., Art Museum,*
*gift of Mr. and Mrs. Albert W. Rice*

**b** John Smibert
Richard Bill, about 1740
*oil on canvas  50¼ × 40¼ in.*
*Chicago, The Art Institute,*
*coll. Friends of American Art*

**c** John James Audubon
Pacific Loon, about 1830
*watercolor  25¼ × 38⅜ in.*
*New York, Historical Society*

**d** Thomas Eakins
The Agnew Clinic, 1889
*oil on cavas  74½ × 130½ in.*
*University of Pennsylvania*

**e** Edward Hicks
The Peaceable Kingdom
*oil on cavas  17½ × 23⅝ in.*
*New York, The Brooklyn Museum*

**c**

Albert Bierstadt depicted the beauty and wild splendor of the Catskills and the valley of the Hudson River around New York. In the Far West the frontier painter, George Caleb Bingham (p. 157), George Catlin, Seth Eastman, and others aimed at a topographical realism with emphasis on the rugged grandeur of mountains, forests, and rivers. George Catlin is particularly notable for his scenes illustrating the life and customs of the retreating Redskin tribes. The wildlife of America was recorded in many exquisite watercolors and sketches by the artist-naturalist John James Audubon (c).

Portraiture in America, although strongly Romantic, was predominantly concerned with exact observation and factual representation. This is particularly evident in the work of the fashionable painters Thomas Sully, Samuel Waldo, George Peter Alexander Healy, and towards the end of the 19th century in the portraits of Thomas Eakins (d). The American scene during this period is also colored by the work of Homer D. Martin, Winslow Homer, and Albert Pinkham Ryder, who had little contact with current European movements and showed strong features of individualism.

Among the most famous of American painters are the expatriates who worked in Europe into the 20th century—James Abbott McNeill Whistler, Mary Cassatt, and John Singer Sargent.

Parallel with these mainstream developments throughout the 19th century was the folk painting practiced by many self-taught and often anonymous artists. They produced landscapes, still-lifes, portraits and other studies in patterned, two-dimensional compositions often strangely moving in their naïveté. The more popular figures in this trend were Lambert Sachs, Joseph H. Davis, and Edward Hicks (e).

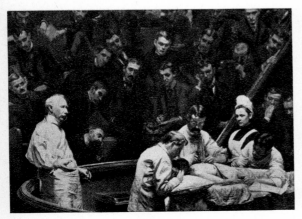

d

e

After about 1830 Romanticism lost its impetus, and in the field of narrative painting the grand and heroic gave place to the anecdotal and the sentimental. Many of the painters of this kind of picture were extremely competent, and their work is now more highly regarded than it used to be. This was the beginning of the age in which works like Delaroche's *Princes in the Tower* (a) caught the popular imagination and had a vast sale as engravings.

The romantic spirit, however, took on a new life in the form of landscape. Quiet landscape painting of a poetic nature is found in the work of the Barbizon School in

**a** Hippolyte Delaroche
The Princes in the Tower, 1831
*oil on canvas    71 × 84 in.*
*Paris, Louvre*

**b** William Mulready
Choosing the Wedding Gown, 1846
*oil on canvas    21 × 18 in.*
*London, Victoria and Albert Museum*

**c** Charles Robert Leslie
Dulcinea del Toboso, 1839
*oil on canvas    12 × 10 in.*
*London, Victoria and Albert Museum*

**d** Thomas Webster
The Village Choir, 1847
*oil on canvas    24 × 36 in.*
*London, Victoria and Albert Museum*

**e** William Collins
As Happy as a King, after 1836
*oil on canvas    27 × 35 in.*
*London, Tate Gallery*

**f** Edward Matthew Ward
The Family of Louis XVI in
the Bastille
*oil on canvas    40 × 50 in.*
*Preston, England, Harris Museum and
Art Gallery*

**g** Ferdinand Waldmüller
Aus dem Prater, 1831
*oil on mahogany    $12\frac{1}{4} \times 10\frac{1}{4}$ in.*
*Hamburg, Kunsthalle*

**h** Théodore Rousseau
Under the Birches, Evening,
about 1842
*oil on wood panel    $16\frac{5}{8} \times 25\frac{3}{4}$ in.*
*Toledo, Museum of Art, Gift
of Arthur J. Secor*

**i** John Linnell
Noonday Rest, 1865
*oil on canvas    36 × 54 in.*
*London, Tate Gallery*

**j** George Inness
Landscape with New England
Elm, 1868
*oil on canvas*
*Philadelphia, Penn., Museum of Art*

**k** Caspar David Friedrich
Two Men Gazing at the Moon,
1819/20
*oil on canvas    12 × 17 in.*
*Dresden, Gemäldegalerie*

**l** Asher Brown Durand
Kindred Spirits, 1849
*oil on canvas    45 × 36 in.*
*New York, Public Library*

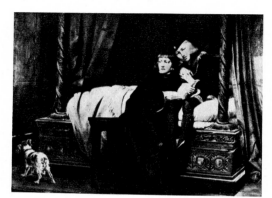

a

b

c

d

e

f

France, in England, in other parts of Europe, and in America. In England, the work of Linnell has its roots in William Blake and Samuel Palmer, but painting elsewhere sometimes has affinities with the German Romantics and in particular with C. D. Friedrich.

g

h

i

j

k

l

## The Pre-Raphaelite Brotherhood

1848 was a year of revolution in Europe. It also marked the establishment in England of a revolutionary art movement, the Pre-Raphaelite Brotherhood. The young men who formed it wished to bring to English painting the purity of spirit and the sincerity of statement which characterized painting in Italy before the time of Raphael. They painted in great detail and in the brightest colors, and very often they selected subjects which had a social message for their own time. In this respect, but in no other, they were in sympathy with the motive which led Courbet to paint his famous *Burial at Ornans* in 1849 (a). Millais' *Christ in the House of His Parents* of 1850 (b) was denounced by Dickens as commonplace and irreverent.

John Ruskin was the only critic who championed the Pre-Raphaelite Brotherhood. Like most art movements it expressed feelings and ideas about painting that were generally "in the air." William Page the American produced a picture of the Pre-Raphaelite type in his portrait of his wife (d).

a

b

c

d

e

f

# Index

Names in italics indicate title of work
Numbers in italics indicate reproductions